ARABS, CHRISTIANS, JEWS

THEY WANT PEACE NOW!

by

James and Marti Hefley

LOGOS INTERNATIONAL
Plainfield, NJ

All scripture verses are taken from the King James Version unless otherwise noted as RSV, Revised Standard Version.

We have written this book as a plea
and a prayer for open-mindedness,
understanding, and compassion for
all those who long for peace in the
land where Judaism, Christianity,
and Islam were born.

Table of Contents

v

1

Arabs, Christians, Jews:
They Want Peace Now!

The younger Arabs stood when the older man strode
into the manager's office at the Grand Palace Hotel in
Amman, Jordan. A Palestinian, he was small with a wiry
build and a thin, immaculately clipped graying mustache.
His military bearing was obvious. His eyes bespoke a
wistful longing.

For an hour he recalled military experiences reaching
across almost thirty years of conflict between Arabs and
Jews: ten years in the British army in Palestine when his
homeland was a British mandate; eighteen more years in
the Jordanian armed forces.

He told of riots provoked by Zionist settlers long before
there was a state of Israel. He spoke of British
insensitivity against his fellow Palestinians. No lights
could burn after sundown. If a Palestinian child happened
to be run over by a jeep, that was of small consequence.

He was only an Arab, and Arabs—to hear the British administrators and the settlers talk—were dirty, lazy wretches who never appreciated anything done for them. And Zionists, many British soldiers believed, had no business coming to Palestine and stirring up the Arabs.

"When the British pulled out in 1948 and the Zionists took over, I fled for my life," the old veteran said. "Thousands upon thousands of us, whose families had tilled the land for hundreds of years, came out. The Jews took our houses and lands and never gave a shilling to anyone.

"I was fortunate. I had military training and could serve in the Jordanian army. There was plenty to do. The fighting never stopped. Peace never came. We Palestinians could never go home. Some of us have accepted Jordanian citizenship. Most are still in the camps, here in Jordan, in Lebanon, in Syria. We have fought four wars and foreigners still occupy our homeland. The killing and the injustices, the raiding and burning goes on. And the world seems not to care.

"Sadat has made his move. He says he wants peace. I believe him. Begin? He was a terrorist himself before he became a politician. I don't trust him. I wish Golda Meir was still in."

His voice softened. His eyes watered. "All my life, I have known war. All my life. And my sons—all their lives they have known war. For my grandchildren, I wish peace."

Peace. Peace. In the land of Moses, Joshua, David, Solomon, Isaiah, and Muhammed, the prophet of Islam. And of Jesus, the Prince of Peace, whose hometown of Nazareth is now divided between Jews and Arabs, with a Communist Palestinian mayor for the Arabs.

Peace. Peace. In the crossroads of the world, land

bridge between three continents, where East meets West, where millions of religious pilgrims come to walk among their holy places, where an oil-thirsty world looks for energy, where the nuclear superpowers scramble for stronger diplomatic footholds.

Peace. Peace. In this land where more wars have been fought and more blood shed than any other place on earth, and where many believe will come the climactic battles at the end of the age when blood will rise to the bridles of horses in the valleys around Jerusalem.

In the kibbutzes, refugee camps, villages, cities, petro-industrial complexes, halls of government, and in mosques, churches, and synagogues, the war-weary people cry for peace.

For themselves and their children.

Now!

Anwar Sadat, a man who prays five times a day, gave many hope. The Egyptian president's bold trip to Jerusalem, made against shouts of "traitor" and "Judas" from his fellow Arabs, came almost three decades after Arab and Jewish armies clashed in the first war over statehood for Zionist Israel. The jet flight from Cairo to Jerusalem took only forty minutes. But it roused the most excitement for peace since the conflict began. Since David Ben-Gurion declared Israel a nation on May 14, 1948, there had been four "just" wars, resulting in thousands of casualties and over two million refugees. Between the wars there had been only tense truces, sometimes policed by nervous UN buffer troops, and shattered by repeated raids, shootings, and constantly escalating guerrilla warfare. All while world leaders talked, the UN debated, and foreign diplomats relayed peace feelers around a circuit of Middle Eastern capitals to Arab and Jewish neighbors who weren't speaking to one another.

Sadat's "sacred mission" stirred pulses in Israel and Arab countries as nothing had in thirty years. Egyptians waved banners in Cairo: SADAT, GOD IS WITH YOU. WE ARE WITH YOU. A poll showed 86 per cent of Americans believing that Sadat's initiative had increased the chance of peace; 40 per cent of those queried said their impressions of Egypt had improved. Another poll showed 73 per cent of Israelis in favor of giving up territories occupied in the Six-Day War of 1967 in return for genuine peace guarantees from Arab neighbors. The previous January only 25 per cent had so agreed.

After Sadat's initial trip to Jerusalem, the first Israeli negotiators flew to Egypt in a plane marked "Shalom" and "Salaam." Said the chief Israeli delegate Eliahu Ben-Elissar to his Egyptian hosts upon alighting, "We are two ancient lands, two very old peoples, two civilizations, two historic neighbors. We come to renew an age-long relationship." Later he quoted from the prophet Isaiah, whose writings are revered by both Jews and Muslims: "In that day shall Israel be the third with Egypt and with Assyria, even a blessing in the midst of the land: Whom the Lord of hosts shall bless, saying, Blessed be Egypt my people, and Assyria the work of my hands, and Israel mine inheritance" (19:24-25).

Still, there was nervousness among the delegates and the horde of journalists who hovered around. Not because of the Egyptians—but from fear of a terrorist bomb blast.

That evening an American woman, a well-known journalist, was awakened by ticking. She checked her travel alarm. She pressed her ear against the wall. The whole wall seemed to be ticking. She called security and four Egyptians came immediately and began examining her walls with metal detectors and listening devices.

Hotel officials moved her and all other guests out of the wing while the search went on. They stood shivering in a rare Cairo rainstorm and waited. Finally after an hour, the head of security announced, "It was the rain dripping behind the wall."

The talks went on. Begin and Sadat, termed "The Odd Couple" by one writer, conferred. They made separate trips to Washington to talk with Jimmy Carter. They chatted about grandchildren and other lighter matters, but always lurking in the background was the awareness that the talks must not fail. A Cairo editor warned, "If we don't make peace this time, there won't be another bus between Cairo and Jerusalem for a hundred years."

The peace talks snagged over interpretation of the critical UN Resolution 242, passed just after Israel tripled her land area in the 1967 Six-Day War. The resolution called for return of occupied Arab territories. Carter and Sadat said it meant "all" territories taken during that war. Begin said the "all" was open to negotiation. He was willing to return the Sinai and perhaps the Gaza Strip, but not all of the Arab area on the West Bank of the Jordan River which included part of Jerusalem. An Israeli politician explained, "He believes in the West Bank as the critical area of history, theology, and strategy." Another observer said, "Begin believes this is part of the land that is Israel's by divine promise and right."

While the argument continued, Israel opened a new "archaeological dig" at Shiloh, where the Hebrew tabernacle stood during the time of the prophet Samuel. Suspicious journalists found it a civilian settlement in disguise. Sadat's hard-line Arab critics cackled, "We told you so. Begin doesn't intend to give up anything." An

5

Egyptian newspaper declared in an open letter to Begin, "We're not Anti-Semitic. We're Anti-You!"

Then came the Palestinian terrorist suicide mission in March 1978. The Sabbath assault on a bus and autos along the coastal highway to Tel Aviv killed thirty-seven Israelis. It was the worst terrorist attack in Israel's history. "Where are my children, my children?" a woman screamed. "If they're dead," her husband vowed softly, "I'll kill all the Arabs in the world."

Israel responded by invading southern Lebanon where the terrorist camps were located amidst both Lebanese Christian and Muslim villages. Over 100,000 refugees ran ahead of the Israeli armor and infantry. Most escaped with only the clothes on their backs. One village television film showed a stooped, aged woman shuffling through the ruins, her lined face a mask of despair. She had refused to leave.

We in the West saw the pictures and heard the grim commentators. Some of us wept for the innocent victims on both sides. How long, O Lord, how long?

But many of us shrugged and said, "Well, after that attack, the Jews had to do something."

More of us were concerned in 1974 when the countries who helped Israel in the 1973 Yom Kippur War were hit by the Arabs with an oil boycott. We waited in long lines at service stations. Some of us faced prospects of unemployment from the closing down of factories dependent on Arab oil. We looked ahead and didn't like what we saw. A crippled economy. A faltering defense. Vulnerability to Communist attack.

For the first time many Westerners began to take the Arabs seriously. We began reexamining the Hollywood stereotypes of sheiks with harems and terrorist hijackers.

After the boycott was lifted, foreign oil prices increased

twelve times over in eight years. That was a prime factor in unleashing inflation. Ouch! We felt the bite every time we went to the store. And it keeps getting worse.

We heard Arthur Burns, then chairman of the U.S. Federal Reserve Board, say somberly, "No economic event in a long generation, excluding only wartime upheavals, has so seriously disrupted our economy as the manipulation of oil prices. . . . A great cloud of uncertainty now surrounds the economic future of nations around the world."

And what of the Arabs? The Arab oil countries are literally awash in money. Saudi Arabia alone takes in $6.8 million more each hour than it can spend. At this rate, the Saudis can buy all the Rockefeller holdings in six days, all the companies on the New York Stock Exchange in nine years, and all the companies on all the world stock exchanges in fifteen years.

The Arabs have already been buying into British and American companies and banks. A Saudi businessman bailed out President Carter's friend Bert Lance. Arabs are also heavy into land speculation. And perhaps most worrisome of all, the Saudis now own $30 billion in American bonds. With 85 per cent illiteracy, the Saudis now hold the largest trade surplus in the world while the U.S. with only 2 per cent illiteracy holds the largest deficit. This trade deficit, which keeps mounting because of the purchase of foreign oil, contributes heavily to inflation at home and the shrinking dollar abroad. Quips an American official in bitter satire: "We'd better learn something fast before the Arabs get smart."

The drop in the dollar's value is playing havoc with the budgets of American missionary agencies abroad. Fewer missionaries can be supported and fewer projects funded. At the same time Arab oil surpluses are enabling Muslim

7

missionaries to step up their efforts in Africa, Asia, Europe, and even in the United States and Canada.

Besides the financial worries, difficulties in the Middle East and also Africa are giving Western diplomats nightmares. Already four Arab countries and the Palestine Liberation Organization (PLO) are being supplied Communist arms. Had Saudi Arabia's 1978 request to purchase fighter planes been rejected by the U.S. Congress, the oil-rich Saudis might have turned to the Russians.

On another front the Soviets and Cubans are allied with the Ethiopians and apparently moving to control the strategic Horn of Africa. If they are successful, the soft underbelly of the oil-rich Arab kingdoms will be vulnerable to guerrilla attacks, and ultimately a Communist takeover. One Arab country, the People's Democratic Republic of Yemen, already has a Marxist government.

What does it all mean?

Many evangelical Christians see further unfolding of events predicted by the ancient Hebrew prophets. The first two major prophetic happenings have already taken place, they say. These are statehood for Israel, and Israel's capture of the Temple site in Jerusalem and other territory once in the old Hebrew kingdom. They predict that the Jews will shortly start rebuilding the ancient Temple.

They further anticipate the soon rise of Antichrist. They say he is probably alive now. Some speculate that the Western economies will collapse and an economic false messiah will arise in Europe or the United States. He will set up his headquarters in Jerusalem and be attacked by a Communist and Arab alliance. Egypt, some believe, will go to the defense of Israel.

8

Whatever the truth in all this, the prophecy books are in a bull market. And at least one author, whose books have sold 14 million copies, is keeping up well with inflation. He is said to be sinking a part of his royalties into long-term real estate ventures—"for my ministry," he says. He isn't worried. His view of prophecy allows for Christ to return before the "Great Tribulation" sets in under the rule of Antichrist. If this happens, his land ventures won't matter.

Meanwhile the killing goes on, inflation tightens, the dollar shrinks, Christian missionary budgets help fewer people, and the Communists maneuver for greater advantage.

Is there no present solution? Must more innocent civilians die in Israel, Lebanon, Jordan, and elsewhere? Must the Palestinian refugees of thirty years continue without hope of ever returning to the homeland of their forefathers? Must we sit idly by and watch a wheel of prophetic fulfillment turn? Are we helpless to prevent greater suffering which many Christians believe is foreordained by God?

Perhaps we would not be so enamored with our charts and dramatic scenarios of the future if we were in the eye of the storm. If we were Israeli citizens residing near the Lebanon border, within range of PLO guns. Or Palestinian refugees living in makeshift housing, existing on meager UN rations, and terrified that the next Israeli retaliatory raid will kill our children.

It is time that we extend our education on the Bible lands beyond prophetic timetables and the network evening news. Time that we scrutinize the worn fatalistic clichés about Arabs and Jews which dampen hopes for peace.

In succeeding chapters, we will seek to answer

9

questions which have been almost entirely ignored amidst the prophecy speculation and debates.

—Did the trouble between Jews and Arabs start in the family of Abraham? Is the present conflict a continuation of an ancient "feud" between Isaac and Ishmael? Are Arabs cursed to hate Jews?

—Why did first-century Jews really reject Jesus the Messiah? And why did a flourishing Gentile church fail in the Middle East?

—How did Muhammed give birth to Islam, the religion of most Arabs today? What does the Muslim holy book, the Koran, say about Jesus, Christianity, and Jews? Why didn't Muhammed become a Christian?

—How did Islam spread so far and so fast? How did Islamic rulers treat Christians and Jews? How is Arab oil now advancing Islam in Africa, Asia, Europe, and even the United States? Are Arab Muslims now waging a "holy war" against Jews and Christians?

—What have Arabs given to the world besides oil? Has history, as taught in Europe and North America, been slanted against Arabs? Is a new "anti-Semitism" raging against Arabs in the West today?

—Why do Muslim Arabs still frown at the sight of a cross? Although there are reported to be small isolated groups meeting in "fellowships," why is there not a single organized Christian congregation of former Muslims in the Arab world today? What have "Christians" done to make Arabs mistrust them so?

—Was the establishment of the state of Israel a divine miracle of prophecy fulfillment, or a strategem of Zionist dreamers? Why did the native Palestinians fight Jewish settlers? Why did some leading Jews oppose a Jewish state? How did Zionists "work" the American political system to obtain recognition of Israel? Why did the

Palestinians flee Israeli armies? Was Menachem Begin actually a terrorist?

—What is the Palestinian problem? Why do some Palestinians become terrorists? What do they want? Who is Yasser Arafat—Palestinian patriot or cold-blooded killer? What "power" does Arafat hold over Arab nations? Why is Arafat opposed to Sadat's peace mission?

—Whose "side" is God on in the Middle East conflict? How have the biblical notes of a deceased lawyer-turned-preacher named Cyrus Scofield helped Israel? Why do many evangelical Christians believe that God has a special plan for Jews in Israel, while others hold that God's purposes are now being worked out in a spiritual Israel—the Church? Why has the first group succeeded and the second failed in "selling" their beliefs to many evangelical Christians?

—Finally, what are the realistic prospects for peace in the Middle East today? How serious is the threat of a Communist takeover? What is God doing among Muslims, Christians, and Jews? Are there signs of a spiritual awakening? Are Israel and the Arab countries doomed to remain enemies through Armageddon? What is the way to peace?

All hard questions that are not easily answered. But answer them we must if we are to be peacemakers in the sacred land that is holy to Muslims, Christians, and Jews.

They want peace and security now.

2

Are Arabs Cursed to Hate?

The biggest fallacy about the Middle East is the most frequently quoted reason for the conflict between Arabs and Jews. People say it all started from a quarrel between two half-brothers, Isaac and Ishmael. Some quote the respected *Halley's Bible Handbook:* "Abraham was the father of the present Arab world. Rivalry between Isaac and Ishmael has persisted through the centuries in the antagonisms between Jews and Arabs."

In 1947 when Arabs were fighting Jewish settlers in Palestine and the United Nations was struggling with the future of the land that is sacred to Judaism, Christianity, and Islam, a Canadian Presbyterian churchman said the trouble started with Sarah, the wife of Abraham. Wrote T. DeCourcy Rayner in the December 1947 issue of *Moody Monthly:* "Sarah, the wife of Abraham, four thousand years after her death, has presented modern statesmanship with its greatest international problem.

Had Sarah believed God (that she would have a son) there would have been no Palestine problem today. Had she not given her slave girl, Hagar, to Abraham, there would have been no Arabs. Ishmael was born of Abraham and Hagar, and the Arabs have descended from Ishmael. The great Palestinian problem of 1947 is that of Arab versus Jew. The dead hands of Sarah are still active."

Twenty-seven years later, an American newspaper correspondent said of the family fuss: "All this happened nearly four thousand years ago. Can a people hate so long without forgetting why they hate? The Arab can."

The story is pressed further in the belief that Arabs, as descendants of the slave woman Hagar through Ishmael, are cursed, while Jews, as children of Sarah through Isaac, are blessed. The proof text to support this claim is lifted from the New Testament: "For it is written that Abraham had two sons, one by the bondwoman and one by the freewoman. But the son by the bondwoman was born according to the flesh, and the son by the freewoman through the promise. This contains an allegory: for these women are two covenants, one proceeding from Mount Sinai bearing children who are to be slaves; she is Hagar . . ." (Galatians 4:22-24, New American Standard Version). It is seldom noted that Paul was using a common allegory held among first-century Jews to make a spiritual analogy between the old covenant of law and the new covenant of grace.

Were the descendants of Ishmael placed under a perpetual curse and foreordained to hate the children of Isaac, the Jews? Were they foreordained to servitude and poverty? And are the modern Arabs Ishmaelites, as so many people believe?

We should look first at the biblical record and read more closely chapters 16, 17, 18, 21, and 25 of Genesis.

14

Sarah did regret sending Abraham to the servant woman's tent. She was jealous of Hagar and the son she bore Abraham. This jealousy exploded at the weaning of Isaac when she saw the older boy "mocking." His action may have been innocent, but Sarah told Abraham to get rid of both the boy and his mother. Abraham did not have to send them away. He did not want to do it. But God told Abraham to do as Sarah wished. ". . . Hearken unto her voice; for in Isaac shall thy seed be called. And also of the son of the bondwoman will I make a nation, because he is thy seed" (21:12-13). Abraham was thus assured that Hagar and Ishmael would be protected. He gave them bread and water and they left.

When the water was gone and Hagar was in despair, an angel appeared and led them to a well of water. Ishmael subsequently married an Egyptian and was blessed with twelve sons who founded twelve tribes in Arabia (modern Saudi Arabia and surrounding oil states).

The patriarch loved both sons. And the sons evidently loved each other. They joined in burying him many years later in the cave of Machpelah (25:9).

Isaac's immediate descendants are better known to Christians and Jews than Ishmael's, which are also given in Genesis. The story of Jacob and Esau is repeatedly taught in church and synagogue. How Esau, the firstborn, sold his birthright to Isaac for a "mess of pottage." How Jacob then tricked Isaac and received the blessing intended for Esau. How Jacob's twelve sons became the heads of the tribes of Israel. And how Esau fathered the Edomites of Mount Seir (now Jordan) and their many tribes and clans.

Christians and Jews tend to skip over the twelve tribes which Ishmael fathered. They are even less aware of Abraham's six sons through Keturah whom he married after Sarah's death. They headed up tribes in the Sinai region and Arabia.

The sojourn of the family of Jacob in Egypt for four hundred years and their deliverance under Moses is better known. But the significance of Moses' marriage to a daughter of the priest of Midian goes unnoticed. The Midianites were from the union of Abraham and Keturah.

On the way back to Canaan, the Hebrew wanderers ran into more "cousins." These were Moabites, from Moab, grandson of Abraham's nephew Lot. It was on Mt. Pisgah in the land of Moab that Moses died. Many years later a Moabitess, Ruth, came into the lineage of Messiah Jesus when she married the Jew Boaz.

Next door to the Moabites lived the Ammonites, descendants of another son of Lot. God told the Hebrews not to fight these "children of my people," a command also given in respect to Moab.

The Hebrews were commanded to fight the idolatrous natives of Canaan. They were descended from three "waves" of Semitic immigrants who had preceded Abraham from Mesopotamia: Amorites, Canaanites (also called Phoenicians), and Aramaeans.

The Amorites had once been ruled by Hammurabi, the famous lawgiver. They may have also built the Tower of Babel.

The Canaanites, or Phoenicians, occupied great city states along the Mediterranean coast. Skilled navigators, they circumnavigated Africa and ventured across the Atlantic. Ancient Phoenician inscriptions were recently uncovered in the American Ozarks. The Phoenicians were also renowned for glassmaking, but their greatest achievement was an alphabet. They probably developed their twenty-two consonantal letter sounds from hieroglyphic picture writing, examples of which have been found in the turquoise mines of the Sinai.

The Aramaeans, who lived in territory now within Lebanon and Syria, were the first to adapt the Phoenician alphabet to a Semitic language, Aramean. From the Aramean model came Assyrian, Armenian, Hebrew, and the principal tongues of India.

The Hebrews brought the worship and laws of one God to a land pervaded by decadent idolatry and sexual license expressed in orgiastic temple ceremonies. In desperate times children were even sacrificed by parents to appease their idols. The covenant Hebrew people were ordered to utterly destroy every vestige of idolatry.

The Hebrews made great gains under the leadership of godly Joshua. Then they broke their covenant with Jehovah by yielding to pagan ways and intermarrying with idolaters. After Solomon's death the Hebrew kingdom split in half. The northern part, Israel, fell to the Assyrians in 722 B.C. The southern portion, Judah, surrendered to the Babylonians in 586 B.C. Babylon was in turn conquered by Persia, Persia by Greece, and Greece by Rome.

Through this long march of history, as empires rose and fell, many of the ancient peoples lost their ancestral identity. What then of the children of Isaac and Ishmael?

The descendants of Isaac, the Jews, hardly kept their race pure. Solomon, for example, had a thousand women in his harem, and many were foreigners. Galilee in the time of Jesus had a notoriously mixed population, causing Nathanael to ask rather contemptuously about Jesus, "Can there any good thing come out of Nazareth?" (John 1:46). Jesus himself was not of pure-blood Hebrew ancestry. There was a Moabitess (Ruth) and a Hittite (Bathsheba, the wife of David) in his mother's line.

The children of Ishmael appear to have kept their line

more pure because they lived in the isolated deserts of Arabia between the Persian Gulf and the Red Sea. But some of them intermarried and converted to Judaism. Among the foreign Jews who heard Peter preach at Pentecost were Arabians.

During the next nineteen hundred years most Ishmaelites and other tribal families of Arabia continued to live in relative isolation, much as they did in the time of Moses and Joshua. Since the discovery of oil wealth underneath the desert sands, they have been slowly modernizing. Their young men work in the oil fields and refineries and on construction projects. Their grandchildren attend universities and some go abroad to earn doctorates.

Ancient Arabia, which never was one nation, is now divided into Saudi Arabia, the two Yemens, Oman, Qatar, Bahrain, and the United Arab Emirates, most of Jordan and a small portion of Iraq. Much of the land is still sparsely settled. All of these countries combined contain only about 20 per cent of the Arab Middle Eastern population. And only a portion of this 20 per cent can be properly called Ishmaelites.

These Ishmaelites and their cousins are certainly not languishing in servitude and poverty. They enjoy the highest per capita annual income of the Middle East. (In one city, university students eat at the local Hilton, with their government picking up the tab!) They will soon be the richest people of the world. Already the average income of citizens of the Arab Emirates is almost double that of Americans.

Do they hate Jews? Again, a stereotype is found wanting. All Arab nations except the tiny People's Democratic Republic of Yemen (the only Marxist country in the Middle East) are moderates in the struggle against

Israel. The so-called Arab hard-line states—Syria, Iraq, Libya, and Algeria—are peopled by an ethnic goulash that defies identification.

The Isaac-Ishmael story is true. But the *application* tacked on by superficial, quick-on-the-draw interpreters is both nonbiblical and patently false.

What then makes an Arab an Arab?

Not race. The Middle Eastern peoples, as we have seen, are descended from a virtual mish-mash of ancients—Aramaeans, Amorites, Phoenicians, Edomites, Ammonites, Midianites, Ishmaelites, Philistines, Syrians, Assyrians, and many others. All of these groups have mixed and intermarried through conquests and political alliances.

Not Islam, though the religion which Muhammed founded, as we shall see in later chapters, is a powerful force in the Arab world, and most Arabs are Muslims.

Not nationhood, for the Arab world covers twenty-two nations and stretches over four thousand miles across North Africa and the Middle East, from Morocco on the Atlantic to Oman's protrusion into the warm Indian Ocean. Cross-directionally, Arab lands run from the Syrian and Iraqi borders with Turkey and Iran respectively to Sudan, which drops deep into the African territory. Turkey and Iran (ancient Persia) are predominantly Muslim but are not considered Arab countries.

There are also sizeable colonies of Arabs living abroad. Around two million Arabs reside in the United States with the strongest concentrations in Detroit, Los Angeles, Houston, Chicago, and New York City. Three of the best known Arab-Americans are entertainer Danny Thomas, U.S. Senator James Abourezk (Dem., South Dakota), and UPI White House Correspondent Helen

Thomas. Thousands of Arab-Americans are Christians. Four Arab Christian leaders are: Dr. John Haggai, a world missionary statesman; Sam Moore, president of Thomas Nelson, Inc., a large evangelical publishing house; Anis Shorrosh, a well-known Southern Baptist evangelist; and Dr. Bahjat Batarseh, who is affiliated with Elim Bible Institute in Lima, New York, and has a ministry to charismatic Christians of all denominations. Dr. Haggai is of Syrian background, Moore was born in Lebanon, Shorrosh is a Palestinian from Nazareth, and Dr. Batarseh is a Jordanian.

Conversely, sizeable minorities of non-Arabs live in Arab countries. A million Kurds are native to Iraq. And at least 200,000 Jews are scattered over the Arab Middle East.

Nor is culture a universal mark of being Arab. Some cultural commonalities do exist. For example, Arab hospitality to strangers stems from the code of the desert which requires that every visitor, even an enemy, be welcomed with *"As-salaam alaykum"* ("Peace be unto you") and be treated and protected as an honored guest. The Arab visitor will not be questioned about his wife, nor will he presume to inquire about his host's spouse. And he will be careful about admiring objects in his host's house, for he knows that whatever he admires will be offered to him.

There are also vast differences among Arab subcultures. The Bedouins crossing the desert on camels are popular for tourist brochures. Contrary to popular belief, these modern nomads do not wander aimlessly about. They know exactly where they're going. Some Bedouin families have followed the same migratory routes for centuries.

The Bedouin clans have their own legal structures.

Each clan is required to defend its own members. When one is dishonored, the entire group feels dishonored and duty bound to execute justice upon the evildoer.

But not all Arabs outside cities travel by camel. The Marsh Arabs of southern Iraq move among their artificial islands on canoes. They raise water buffaloes for milk and use dried dung for fuel. These Arabs are worlds apart from the mysterious Druze mountain people of Lebanon and Syria, who follow a strange blend of Islam, Christianity, and paganism. And the Druzes are notably different from Christian Copts in southern Egypt who farm the fertile soil along the banks of the Nile and Yemeni farmers who till terraced slopes of grain, fruit, and coffee where tradition says the Queen of Sheba once reigned.

Volumes could be written showing the complexities of Arabs. The only unifying identification of Arabness remains the Arabic language.

Arabs—whether Egyptian, Saudi, Iraqi, Muslim, Christian, or even Jew—are people whose first language is Arabic.

Arabic, the Semitic cousin of Hebrew, is directly descended from the ancient Aramean language. Aramean split into eastern and western dialects. The western group further divided into Aramaic, Nabatean, and Syriac. (Several chapters of the Old Testament were originally written in Aramaic, which was probably also the language Jesus spoke in first-century Palestine.) The eastern side split into Syriac and Mandiac. Syriac developed into Arabic.

Since Arabic is also the language of the Koran and Islam, it carries numerous built-in attitudes and expressions of affection. An Arab stranger may be greeted by a stranger on a Cairo bus as *ya aini* ("my eye") or *ya akhi* ("my brother"). *Insh Allah* ("if God wills") is added to every spoken plan. This reflects the Muslim belief that nothing is inevitable or fixed; everything is subject to an all-governing Providence.

Home and village Arabic varies from region to region. Egyptians, for example, pronounce the first name of Egypt's former president "Gamal," while Iraqis pronounce the name "Jamal."

Literary, formal (classical) Arabic is the same everywhere. What a broadcaster says in Beirut about American foreign policy is understood perfectly in Cairo or Casablanca.

When Arabs speak formally, they frequently ascend into metaphor and hyperbole. Those figures of speech are found in the New Testament. Jesus spoke of a faith that moves mountains—a metaphor—and the difficulty of a camel going through a needle's eye—perhaps also a metaphor which some scholars believe refers to a small pedestrian gate in the wall around Jerusalem.

Arab hyperbole puzzles Westerners. When the United States canceled aid for Egypt's Aswan Dam project, President Gamal Nasser responded, "Let them choke on their fury." He actually meant the much softer, "Let them jump in the lake." More applicable to the current scene is a vow once made by Arab hard-liners to "drive Israel into the sea." Western supporters of Israel visualized a huge army of vengeful Arabs driving the entire Israeli population into the Mediterranean to drown. These Arabs meant that they intended to defeat Israel and establish a homeland for dispossessed Palestinian refugees. They frequently said that a Jewish minority was living peacefully in Palestine before Israel became a state, and that Jews would still be welcome in a Palestinian state.

More moderate Arabs, such as Egypt's Sadat, Jordan's

Hussein, and Saudi Arabia's King Khalid, although they have not so proclaimed, are even willing to accept the existence of Israel. However, they are united with the hard-liners that Israel must return the territories occupied in 1967 and restore to the Palestinians a homeland.

From the Arabs' point of view, this is not because Israel is Jewish, as we shall see in later chapters. The Arabs see Israel as an extension of foreign colonialism, given land stolen by Britain and armed by the United States.

The much talked about squabble in the family of Abraham has little to do with this conflict that has threatened world peace for over thirty years—except that it has made millions believe there is no solution and that Arab and Jewish enmity is predestined to continue until the end of the world.

3

What Happened to Christianity in the Middle East?

The myths which Westerners hold of Middle Eastern peoples are legion. Every Arab and Jewish diplomat and tourist guide has a bittersweet story to tell. The following true incident is illustrative.

An American lady attended a reception at an Arab embassy in old Jerusalem when it was still under Arab control. She was introduced to Anton Atallah—lawyer, banker, then foreign minister of Jordan, and a lay leader in the Greek Orthodox church. "Dr. Atallah is a prominent Arab," she was told.

"Ohh, a real Arab!" she gushed. "How interesting. And how many wives do you have?"

Dr. Atallah's eyes twinkled. He was accustomed to such questions. "Oh, just one, thank you. And unlike some Americans, she's the same one I married years ago. That's the way it usually is around here—with Muslims and, of course, among Christians."

"Ohh, so you're a Christian Arab?" she continued without blinking. "And what mission were you converted by?"

"By no mission, madam. My ancestors were Christians long before the faith came to your country. Indeed, my own congregation traces its succession to apostolic times."

She couldn't believe it.

Such lack of understanding is not surprising. For most Christians in the West, the history of the Bible lands stops when the apostle John was exiled on the Island of Patmos and does not resume until 1948 when Israel became a state. Some are aware that their churches have missionaries in Israel and the Arab countries. They presume that a small minority of Arabs have been converted under these missionaries.

Thus the following facts are astonishing:

The oldest churches in the world are in the Middle East.

From 10 to 15 per cent of all present-day Arabs are at least nominal Christians. Some are in church bodies which date their tradition to apostolic times. Their ancestors were among the first Gentile converts of the first Christian missionaries.

Five million Coptic Christians in Egypt believe that their church was founded by Mark, the author of the second Gospel and companion of Paul during part of the apostle's first missionary journey. The Copts, who also constituted the established church in Ethiopia before the Marxist revolution there, believe that Mark founded the first Coptic (Copt means Egyptian) church in Alexandria. They identify the "Babylon" which sent greetings in the closing verses of Peter's first Epistle with a church founded by Mark in old Cairo. Whether true or not, the

Egyptian church was probably flourishing by around A.D. 100.

The oldest church sanctuary is claimed by Armenian Christians who number about 300,000 in Iran. Their "Black Church" (so named because of the color of the stone used in its construction) is named for the apostle Thaddeus who, according to Armenian tradition, brought Christianity to Persia (modern Iran).

The first church congregation was, of course, at Jerusalem. The second was at Antioch, a city in southern Turkey, lying just above the border of Syria. Here the disciples of Jesus were first called Christians and from here the missionary movement to the Gentiles was launched. The major thrust was north into present Turkey and west to Greece and Italy, but by the second century there were churches all across what is now called the Arab world. The Church was then divided into three patriarchates or bishoprics at Rome, Antioch, and Alexandria. During the next two centuries, Christianity kept spreading. At the Council of Nicea, A.D. 325, there were six bishops from Arabia where there are no organized Christian church structures today.

These early churches were almost entirely Gentile in contrast to the first church at Jerusalem which had been almost entirely Jewish. The same pattern exists today. There is not one congregation of Christian Jews in Israel or elsewhere in the Middle East, although there are some Messianic Jewish Christians who worship with Gentile believers.

How did it happen that Jesus became the "Gentiles' Messiah"? How did the Church change from a Jewish to a Gentile constituency? And how did the Gentile church in the Bible lands lose its spiritual power and split apart, leaving the way open for Islam to conquer this historic area?

The answers to these questions are essential to understanding the trail of tragedy in the Bible lands which continues to this day.

Jesus was a Jew. He observed all the tenets of Judaism. He astounded Jews with His miracles. And He excited and infuriated many Jews by declaring that God loved not only Jews but Gentiles also.

The battle began in His home synagogue at Nazareth when He was invited to read from the Hebrew Scriptures. He chose selections from Isaiah 58:6 and 61:1-2: "The Spirit of the Lord is upon Me, because He anointed Me to preach the gospel to the poor. He has sent Me to proclaim release to the captives, and recovery of sight to the blind, to set free those who are downtrodden, to proclaim the favorable year of the Lord." Then He announced, "Today this Scripture has been fulfilled in your hearing" (Luke 4:18, 19, 21, New American Standard Version).

The room buzzed with questions. "Is this not Joseph's son?" people asked in amazement (v. 22).

He replied with illustrations from the Hebrew Scriptures that proved Jehovah was no nationalistic God for Jews. A Gentile in Sidon had been fed miraculously while Jewish widows were left to die of starvation, he recalled. Naaman the Syrian leper had been healed, while Jewish lepers had gone untouched (vv. 25-27).

Their reaction indicated how completely possessed they were by racial pride. Who was this carpenter's son, this miracle worker, to say that God loved unclean, uncircumcised, idolatrous Gentiles as much as He did Jews, even to the point of sometimes helping Gentiles first! They had wanted Him to perform miracles as He had done elsewhere. Instead, He had revealed their sin from their own Scriptures. Consumed with anger they pushed

Him out of the building and outside Nazareth to a precipice, apparently intending to hurl Him over the brink. To their chagrin He slipped through the crowd and escaped unharmed (vv. 28-30).

This racial pride was the basis for one of the saddest observations in the New Testament, which came at the beginning of Jesus' public ministry: "He came unto his own, and his own received him not" (John 1:11).

From this time He seemed to go out of His way to show that He was no racial Messiah.

Take His deliberate trip across Samaria, which devout Jews avoided because of longstanding racial prejudices against the inhabitants. The trouble dated from the time when Ezra and Nehemiah had led a remnant of Jews back from Babylonian captivity. They were confronted by the children of mixed marriages between pagans and Jews who had remained in the land. These hybrids actually professed to worship Jehovah and had the audacity to want to help rebuild the sacred Temple. Their leader was Manasseh, son of the hereditary Jewish high priest. There was an angry confrontation and uproar. Manasseh was expelled. The Samaritans were blacklisted. The region became a haven for castoffs and apostates, much as Rhode Island was a refuge for nonconformists fleeing oppressive church-state regimes in other American colonies.

The animosity between Jews and Samaritans boiled for the next four and one-half centuries. Around 6 B.C. Samaritans slipped into the Temple in Jerusalem and scattered human bones around the porches of the holy place. Jewish authorities declared all Samaritans accursed and pronounced their food to be as unclean as swine's flesh.

Imagine the provocation, then, of Jesus' deliberately leading His disciples across the territory of the hated racial outcasts. Imagine the resentment created when it became known that He had sent His disciples into the Samaritan town of Sychar to buy food while He rested at a well. Imagine the scandal caused when it was later disclosed that He had talked to a woman, a Samaritan, one living openly in adultery, and announced to her that He was the promised Messiah, an announcement He had not made to Jews. A devout male Jew in that era thanked God every day that he was not born a woman or a Gentile. Being born a Samaritan woman and then becoming an adulteress was too revolting to mention.

This was not all. Later Jesus had the brazenness to illustrate neighborliness by telling how a Samaritan had aided a Jewish crime victim after a priest and a Levite had passed the unfortunate man by.

There were other reasons why most of the Jewish leadership rejected Jesus. He exposed their sins to the common people. He demanded justice. He aroused such a following that they feared the Romans would think a revolution was brewing and would brutally "restore order." Most of all they hated Him for claiming to be God in the flesh. How could such a race-mixer, rabble-rouser, and revolutionist be God!

They schemed and planned and manipulated His death by Roman crucifixion.

He didn't stay dead. He arose from the dead and commanded His disciples to "Go . . . teach all nations."

The disciples still hadn't grasped the universality of His love. Nor did they understand the full meaning and purpose of His atoning death on the cross. Surely now that He has demonstrated His power, they thought, He will start setting up the earthly kingdom foretold by David and Solomon. Their only question was, "When?"

"It is not for you to know the times or the seasons, which the Father hath put in his own power," Jesus replied forcefully (Acts 1:7). Then he turned them to spiritual reality. "And, behold, I send the promise of my Father upon you: but tarry ye in the city of Jerusalem, until ye be endued with power from on high. . . . But ye shall receive power, after that the Holy Ghost is come upon you: and ye shall be witnesses unto me both in Jerusalem, and in all Judea, and in Samaria, and unto the uttermost part of the earth" (Luke 24:49; Acts 1:8).

Chapters 2-6 of the Acts of the Apostles tell the dynamic story: the descent of the Spirit at Pentecost; three thousand Jews converted from fifteen nationalities, including Arabians and Egyptians; the Church which broke bread and worshiped in home fellowships and saw new believers added daily; the fanatical opposition of die-hard religious authorities who had Peter and John thrown in jail; healing miracles; deliverance from prison in answer to prayer.

Then came Stephen's dramatic speech at his trial, the same message Jesus had given in the synagogue at Nazareth: God is not nationalistic. Worship is not centered in a temple. God, as Solomon reminded, can't be boxed into a house made with hands. After Stephen charged the religious leaders with "always" resisting the Holy Spirit "as your fathers did," and of killing the Just One (Jesus), they stoned him to death, just as they had wanted to kill Jesus three years before at Nazareth. It was racial pride. Stephen was killed not for following Jesus, but for the Messiah's love for all people.

After Stephen's death, the evangelization of Gentiles began. First it was Jewish proselytes, then God-fearing

Gentile inquirers into Judaism, then raw pagans.

This extension of the gospel divided the followers of Messiah Jesus. "Judaizers" said Gentiles couldn't be considered saved until they converted to Judaism. Broader minds disagreed: ". . . Why . . . put a yoke upon the neck of the disciples, which neither our fathers nor we were able to bear? But we believe that through the grace of the Lord Jesus Christ we shall be saved, even as they" (Acts 15:10-11).

The dispute troubled the Church for decades. Judaizers trailed Paul and other missionaries from one Gentile city to another, telling new believers that they had heard an incomplete gospel. Paul wrote letters back (particularly the Epistle to the Galatians) charging that the Judaizers "would pervert the gospel of Christ" (Galatians 1:7).

There were simply more Gentile converts than the Judaizers could handle. They and other nationalistic Jews, who could accept Jesus only as *their* Messiah, began separating themselves from other believers. When Paul died about A.D. 66 the Church was largely composed of Gentiles.

Judaism fell on much harder times after a Roman army, led by Titus, marched on Jerusalem to put down a rebellion. The revolt had been in protest of sacrilege of the Temple by the Roman procurator. The Romans besieged and burned the city in A.D. 70, fulfilling a prediction made by Jesus almost forty years before.

Once more, in 113, Jewish zealots tried to throw off the yoke of Rome. They rallied behind an acclaimed military messiah named Simon bar Kochba. This time the Romans devastated the ancient land promised to Abraham. The Jewish population was practically wiped out. Jews would not try to reclaim the land for another nineteen centuries.

There had long been Jewish colonies in foreign cities.

Taking a lesson from the brutality of the Romans, they pursued quietness. The Romans left them alone.

The Christians did not remain quiet. Shorn of narrow nationalism, wave after wave of missionaries pushed Christianity to the outermost limits of the Roman Empire. They established strong churches in cities where Christianity is weak and ineffectual today, and in some places nonexistent.

The Roman dictators and their bureaucratic and military infrastructures could not stamp out the fire. For every martyr thrown to the lions or burned for refusing to worship Lord Caesar, a hundred more believers seemed to spring up. By the fourth century around 20 per cent of the empire's population was Christian.

Early in this century the emperor himself was converted. Constantine announced he had seen a flaming cross in the sky emblazoned with the command, "In this sign you shall conquer." The next year he proclaimed Christianity a "lawful religion."

The new "brother" in the palace quickly made his power known. He proclaimed the Christian "sabbath" as an official day of rest. He convened the great church Council of Nicea which declared that Jesus was "very God of very God." This resulted in Jews being branded as "God's murderers" and becoming the object of discriminatory actions. New synagogues were prohibited. Conversion to Judaism became a penal offense. Intermarriage between Jews and Christians was punishable by death.

Christianity became more centralized around Rome, more bureaucratic, and more subject to influence peddling. Bishoprics became more powerful and political. Having the right connections counted far more than piety, morality, and spiritual knowledge.

The church was further weakened in 395 when the

empire split between east and west at the death of Emperor Theodosius I. One son, Honorius, ruled the Latin-speaking west. Another son, Arcadius, presided over the Greek-speaking east. He established the capital of his Byzantine Empire at Constantinople (modern Istanbul, Turkey). But the central headquarters of the church remained at Rome, even though the western empire was beginning to disintegrate in anarchy.

During these tumultuous times the church was struggling for doctrinal stability amidst perversions that kept congregations in confusion. Many were spin-offs of a Greek philosophy called Gnosticism (possessing knowledge and spiritual insight) that taught a line of spiritual deities, good and bad, and promised salvation through occult knowledge. With the dualism in deities, the Gnostics further divided man into flesh and spirit. The system inspired both extreme asceticism and extreme license.

A Christian variety of Gnosticism taught an Old Testament Creator God who had cared only for Israel and a New Testament God of love and mercy, whom Christ revealed. This was promoted by Marcion, who had been excommunicated from the church for heresy. Marcion rejected the Old Testament and issued his own New Testament containing only ten of Paul's Epistles and an edited version of Luke's Gospel. Because of Marcionism, church councils were forced to decide on the official canon of the twenty-seven New Testament books which we have today.

Doctrinal disputes over the nature of Christ had not settled. If Jesus was God, should Mary be called "Mother of God"? Nestorius, the patriarch at Constantinople, said no. The Father had begotten Jesus as God, he said, while Mary had only given birth to the Savior as a man. Cyril of

Alexandria called this heresy and appealed to Pope Celestine I.

In a related controversy, other prelates wrangled over the idea that Christ had been born human and the Son of God had assumed the flesh of Mary's son and absorbed it into His divinity. This was called Monophysitism—Christ is of one divine nature.

A church council met at Ephesus in 431 but couldn't settle the issue. Twenty years later prelates tried again at the Council of Chalcedon, a sleepy little port city across the Bosphorous Strait from Constantinople. The majority voted that Jesus Christ was true God and true man, having two distinct natures that are inseparably joined in one person and partaking of one divine substance.

Nestorius was deposed to Antioch. A number of church leaders and congregations remained loyal to him. These Nestorians later sent the first missionaries to China. They survive in the Middle East today as the Assyrian church.

The Monophysites were subsequently excommunicated by the pope and pronounced accursed by the eastern emperor. They divided into factions from which three other major church bodies continue today in the Middle East, North Africa, and in smaller communities elsewhere. The Coptic church is in Egypt and Ethiopia. A second branch, known as the Jacobite church, endures in Egypt and Iraq. A third continues as the Armenian church in Iraq, Iran, Turkey, and Soviet Armenia.

An attempt to reconcile Monophysites and Chalcedonians led only to more quarreling and charges of heresy. A compromise statement, called Monothelitism, said that one Christ had worked the human and the divine elements of His nature through divine-human energy. Objectors rammed through this statement at another council: Christ has "two natural wills . . . not contrary one to the other. . . . His human will follows, not as resisting or reluctant, but rather as subject to his divine and omnipotent will."

The Monothelitists would not accept this and broke away to form a church named for their leader, John Maron. In the twelfth century the Maronites returned to the fold of Rome, and were allowed to retain their ritual and married priesthood. Modern Maronites comprise almost half the population of Lebanon and also have congregations in Syria and Cyprus.

These doctrines were much closer to orthodoxy than other heresies that troubled Christianity in the Middle East in the seventh century. A faction of Gnostics, called Docetists, said Christ couldn't possibly have had a body because, (1) absolute cannot unite with finite, and (2) matter, including human flesh, is evil and always in conflict with spirit. Christ had only seemed to be a real man.

Ebionites swung to the other extreme. They said Christ was truly a man who had not been virgin born. His messianic work was only that of prophet and teacher.

Extra-canonical scriptures continued to circulate. The "Gospel of Thomas" told of a five-year-old Jesus miraculously making twelve sparrows from clay. The "Acts of John" had the apostle John exorcising a plague of bedbugs from his bed. The "Acts of Paul" told how Paul had baptized a lion. The "Acts of Peter" described how a dry sardine had been made to swim again.

Self-ordained prophets and preachers carried these and other wild stories from place to place. Not many congregations were grounded in sound doctrine as evangelical Christians understand it today.

The stage was set for the advent of a new and vigorous

prophet who would step into the doctrinal confusion and spiritual vacuum. He would claim a once-for-all revelation from God, superseding all previous Jewish and Christian writings. He would be the apostle of Islam, the dominant religion of the Arab world today.

4

Muhammed's Legacy

Five times a day. Beginning at dawn. In every time zone. On every continent. In Cairo, Jerusalem, Damascus, Baghdad, Beirut, Amman, Lahore, Kabul, London and thousands of other cities, towns, and villages where live 700 million Muslims.

From the high, slender, minaret tower that ascends from every mosque, the muezzin calls Allah's faithful to prayer.

"*Allahu akbar! Allahu akbar!* God is greater! God is greater!

"There is no God but God.

"And Muhammed is the messenger of God."

King and soldier, corporate czar and shepherd, oil sheik and taxi driver answer the call. The prayer mat is stretched towards holy Mecca. The worshiper removes his shoes, covers his head, and prostrates himself in prayer. If prayer is not possible at the appointed time—for instance, if the oil sheik is about to close a multimillion-dollar deal or the cabby is driving a fare—the Muslim knows Allah (God) understands and will not be offended if he postpones the duty to later.

"In the name of God, most Merciful and Compassionate," the Muslim always begins. "Praise be to God, the cherisher and sustainer of the world, Most Merciful and Compassionate Master of the Day of Judgment, Thee alone do we worship, and only Thine aid do we seek. Show us the straight way, the way of those on whom Thou has bestowed Thy grace, those whose portion is not wrath and who go not astray."

Then continuing with any other prayers and portions of the Koran he may remember, and always concluding by asking God to "bless Muhammed and his people as Thou hast blessed Abraham and his people."

The traveler in a Muslim community cannot miss the call to prayer. In more conservative areas, such as Saudi Arabia, religious police enforce the closing of shops at the appointed prayer times. And one who happens to be in a Muslim country during the fast month of Ramadan (which varies because of the lunar calendar observed) will not take a devout Muslim to lunch. From dawn to sunset, the faithful abstain from food, liquids, smoking, and sex. (Alcoholic beverages are taboo at all times.)

Ramadan is the month from which Muslims date the first divine revelation to their prophet Muhammed. Islamic history locates the place of revelation in a cave on Mt. Arafat (in Arabic, "mountain of mercy") overlooking the narrow, dry stony Hijaz valley in Arabia. In this valley is the sacred city of Mecca, the place of pilgrimage for every Muslim in the world. Only the subjects of Allah may come to Mecca which is in Saudi Arabia, one of the most conservative Islamic kingdoms in the world. Only they may visit the sacred mountain and also walk through the grand Haram (meaning "holy and inviolable") Mosque, complete seven circuits around the inner court, then enter the black-robed, cubed Kaaba which holds Islam's most sacred shrine. This is the celebrated Black Stone, a meteorite which Islam says the Angel Gabriel gave to Abraham and on which the Great Ancestor made his first sacrifice to the One God. It is kissed smooth from millions of lips.

Here in this dry desert valley, Muhammed founded the religion which is now the faith of the majority in forty-seven countries. He is not worshiped as a god. That would be blasphemy. He is remembered as the last and greatest of the monotheistic prophets, the one to whom Allah dictated, through Gabriel, the sacred scripture which Muslims call simply the Koran—"the reading." And his name is today the most common first name in the world.

He was born Muhammed ibn Abdallah ibn Abdal-Muttallah ibn Hashem el-Quaraysh about A.D. 570. Ibn means "son of" and Quaraysh is his tribe. The Quaraysh was one of dozens of tribes in Arabia but the most prominent in Mecca. Members claimed descent from Ishmael.

At the time of Muhammed's birth the Quaraysh and other tribes were idolaters. Each tribe had its own pantheon of deities. The chief god of the Quaraysh was named Allah, an Arabic word grammatically incapable of taking a plural, meaning literally "the god." The Quaraysh worshiped Allah as the supreme creator-provider. He had been revered in Arabia for at least eleven hundred years, and was said to have three daughters, all possessing divine powers.

At the center of Mecca was the spacious court on which the various tribes had placed 360 sacred stones and images of their gods. Among the pantheon was the Kaaba, containing the Black Stone along with images of the moon god Hubal and the three daughters of Allah.

Thousands of Arabians came each year to march ritualistically around the Kaaba seven times and then venerate their chosen deities. The Meccan economy was built around the idolatrous worship, and merchants competed for the trade of pilgrims.

Most of the Meccan merchants were Quaraysh. They welcomed the pilgrim idolaters, but not Jews and Christians who lived in the surrounding hills. The monotheists did not buy images. They were forbidden by the second commandment in their Scriptures to make likenesses of their God.

Knowledge of Muhammed's early life is sketchy. It is known that his father was a small merchant and that he died two months after the future prophet's birth. Muhammed's mother also died six months later and the boy was sent to live with his grandfather. The grandfather shortly passed away and an uncle, abu Talib, took in the unfortunate child. Abu Talib was a prominent merchant in Mecca, but he put Muhammed to shepherding his flock.

At twelve Muhammed accompanied his uncle on a buying trip to Syria. Later he made other trips as the representative of a Meccan widow named Khadija, who had a rich inheritance from two husbands. Impressed by his talent, she proposed marriage. They were wed when Muhammed was twenty-five and Khadija forty.

A tradition says he met a Christian monk named Bahira on his first visit to Syria. Another story has a Jewish rabbi for his tutor. Though Jews and Christians were unpopular among his kinsmen, young Muhammed undoubtedly knew some. He certainly became acquainted with Christians and Jews on his trips to Syria.

How much he was influenced by Jews and Christians is hard to say. As manager of his wife's business, he became renowned for honesty. He also donated regularly to the poor. He obtained his wife's permission to free the slaves she had inherited. These were actions that might be expected of a devout Jew or Christian, and that could have made him disliked by his fellow merchants.

Why then didn't Muhammed accept Christianity or Judaism? For Judaism there might have been ethnic reasons. Jews were divided among factions and clannish among their respective groups. They commonly made much of their ancestries and special privileges as God's chosen people. And Jews were not zealous for converts, either.

Christians taught that their gospel was for everybody. In the fellowship of Christ there was supposed to be no special race or status. What kept Muhammed from becoming a Christian?

We can only speculate. The Church was divided. The squabbles over the nature of Christ were known throughout Arabia. Muhammed, to some extent, must have been aware of these divisions and may have thought that many Christians believed in three gods, Father, Son, and Holy Spirit. It must have been hard for him to understand how Christ had been born human and become divine, as the Copts of Egypt and Abyssinia (Ethiopia) believed.

The Arabian tribes were always quarreling and involved in petty wars. Christians were little better. Their spiritual leaders were embroiled in politics and some were converting by the sword. Christian Abyssinia

(Ethiopia) was pushing into Arabia, taking advantage of the divisions among the idolatrous tribes. The year of Muhammed's birth a band of Arabians from Mecca had retaliated by polluting the Abyssinian cathedral at Sana. The Abyssinians countered by attacking Mecca. They were driven off by an epidemic of "small pebbles" (smallpox) which the Meccans saw as a providence from their gods. But the Abyssinians regrouped and kept trying to add to their territory.

Meanwhile, Muhammed was making regular visits to a cave. Sometimes he stayed all night, meditating on the gods, asking the three goddesses in the Kaaba to intercede for him with Allah. In time he concluded that the goddesses were angels and that Allah was the only god.

One night in the year 610 he was praying about what Allah wanted him to do when, according to the Koran, the Angel Gabriel appeared before him and announced:

> Recite: In the name of thy Lord who createth,
> Created man from a clot.
> Recite: And it is thy Lord the Most Bountiful
> Who
> Teacheth by the pen,
> Teacheth man that which he knew not. . . .
> (Koran, Surah 96:1-6)

Shaken, and thinking he had been beset by demons, Muhammed ran home to his wife. Khadija calmed him and suggested he confide in a relative, an old man who knew the Jewish and Christian Scriptures. The man assured him that Allah had indeed given him a message.

Muhammed was by nature reserved and shy. He went back to the cave and received more revelations. A resurrection was coming and after that a judgment rendered on the basis of man's deeds, the voice said. At the judgment every man would receive a list to read aloud. If placed in the right hand, it would be a list of rewards, if in the left, his punishments. The righteous ones would then be transported to a sumptuous shaded paradise where cool waters flowed through gardens of delight. There, they would feast on fruit from tall trees, drink from goblets served by blooming youth, and enjoy spouses kept forever virgin young.

Muhammed was forty years old. He began preaching to his relatives and neighbors. Most paid him little attention at first. There were soothsayers (speakers for the supernatural) in every tribe.

His wife and daughters were his first converts, then his cousin Ali, a freed slave named Zayd, and a wealthy friend named abu Bakr. Muhammed demanded that these and future believers profess faith in the One God, Allah, and submit to his will. From submit Islam takes its name. The consonants "slm" mean submission in the Semitic root form.

The community of Islam grew. The merchants became alarmed as they saw their business in religious relics dropping off. They feared ruin.

They condemned Muhammed's preaching. They tortured slaves who had submitted to Allah's will. Abu Bakr spent a large portion of his fortune buying the freedom of suffering slaves.

Muhammed considered Islam an advancement of Judaism and Christianity. Muslims still do. Because of the persecution, he sent eighty-two men and women to seek refuge among the nearest Coptic church congregation. One of the eighty-two was his own daughter.

The merchants proclaimed a boycott against the

submitters to Allah. The boycott did not hold. But the Prophet was hit hard by two heavy blows. In the year 619 both his wife and his uncle abu Talib died. The uncle's place as head of the clan was taken by his brother abu Lahab, a fanatical opponent of Islam, a relative Muhammed had once cursed.

Then Muhammed shocked the group by claiming that Gabriel had taken him by night to Jerusalem and lifted him to Paradise. They murmured in unbelief until the unshakable abu Bakr stilled their skepticism.

The persecution at Mecca continued. Finally Muhammed sent some families two hundred miles across the desert to Yathrib, a town in a fertile oasis, where there were other converts. On the dark night of September 24, 622 he and the rest followed, fleeing Mecca on camels. This Hegira (flight) marks the first year of the Muslim calendar.

Allah's followers at Yathrib offered their homes for worship, but the Prophet said Allah would lead his camel to a chosen spot. The beast reportedly stopped and knelt near a small shed used for storing dates. Here the community built the world's first mosque. The interior was plain and modest. There were no images or drawings on the wall. All seats were the same and none were reserved for dignitaries. All were equal in the brotherhood, Muhammed said.

As Muhammed continued to announce revelations, the ritual and beliefs of Islam kept developing. They were both similar to and different from Judaism and Christianity. At Mecca Muhammed's people had prayed twice daily toward Jerusalem. At Yathrib he added a third prayer at midday, conforming to the Jewish schedule. The Jews blew the ram's horn in summons to prayer. Christians banged great wooden clappers.

Muhammed appointed a human caller. The first was a black convert from Abyssinia named Bilal. Islam's weekly services were on the Jewish sabbath. The form was much like the Jews and Christians followed: prayer led by a male member of the congregation, a reading from the writing which would later become the Koran, and a sermon which Muhammed often gave himself. There was no priesthood or ministry in Islam.

The Muslims changed the name of Yathrib to Medina ne-Nabi, "city of the Prophet." Today it is reverenced as the second holiest city in Islam.

The Jews at Medina had been proclaiming the coming of a messiah who would stamp out idolatry. Muhammed had hopes they would accept him as the expected one. Instead, the Jewish rabbis argued with him on various doctrines and sought to correct his gaps of Old Testament knowledge. Muhammed declared that the Jews had fallen away from the true faith and twisted the Scriptures to conform with their own opinions.

Abraham, he declared, was the founder of the true faith of Islam. Abraham had founded the sanctuary in Mecca for his son Ishmael and established the pilgrimage which the idolaters had corrupted. As God's prophet, he, Muhammed, had been appointed to complete the revelation begun in Old Testament times.

To ease tensions, Muhammed hammered out an agreement with the Jews. Muslims and Jews would both live under his laws and customs. They would join in defense against any attack by idolaters.

The alliance soon began breaking down. The Muslims asserted civil authority over the Jews. The Jews feared losing their freedom as well as people to Islam and conspired with the Meccan merchants who were now avowed enemies of Muhammed. When Muhammed learned about this, he expelled the most troublesome Jewish tribe. He changed the Muslim day of public prayers from Saturday to Friday, and prayed towards Mecca instead of Jerusalem.

The revelations kept coming. Five pillars of obedience became a distinguishing characteristic of the new faith. Profession of faith in God's oneness and Muhammed as his messenger headed the list. Second was the obligation of prayer, at the now appointed five times a day. Third was alms. An alms tax, *zakah*, of about 2.5 per cent of produce or income for the community became obligatory. A second type of alms, *sadakah*, was to be given voluntarily directly to the poor. Fourth was fasting during the month of Ramadan. Fifth was pilgrimage to Mecca, even though Muslims were banned by the hostile merchants.

The revelations included extensive instruction on marriage and family—all from the male perspective. "One of God's signs," said Muhammed, "is that He created mates for you . . . that you may find rest in them, and . . . between you love and compassion. . . . Marry as pleases you, two, three, or four women: and if you fear that you cannot be equitable, then only one or as many female slaves as your hands may possess" (Koran, Surah 30:20, 4:3). Slavery is today outlawed in Muslim countries, and few Muslim men have more than one wife.

Muhammed lived monogamously before Khadija died. He then took about a dozen wives of various ages. One was the daughter of his old friend abu Bakr. Another was a Christian Copt. Islamic apologists today explain the discrepancy between the Prophet's command and practice by noting that Muhammed married some women in honor of their martyred husbands and others to build ties with powerful families.

A husband was a step above a wife, the Prophet said,

and must provide for her "because God has given the one more strength than the other." But a wife should recognize a certain weakness in men. She should never flaunt her body or dress immodestly outside the house. In any case, a husband was responsible for a wife's conduct, but must not render corporal punishment until all else fails. Adultery could be punished by death.

A husband could divorce a wife by saying that he has lost desire for her. But no wife must ever be sent away without "generosity" and provision made for care of children. And a wife may seek a divorce if her husband has mistreated her.

Still divorce is "the most hateful to God of all the things that He permits," Muhammed said. Muslim leaders today say that the divorce rate is much, much less in Islamic societies than in the "Christian" West.

Muhammed developed in Medina the model for Islamic theocracy. God is the sovereign Head and cannot be divided, numbered or limited. He cannot be known personally nor described by artistry, for that would be idolatry. He can only be praised and adored by names such as the ninety-nine "Beautiful Names" in the Muslim's "rosary."

God does not ordain His decrees because they are just and holy, but because it pleases Him to do so. Thus He can change or rescind them as He desires.

God wills. Man surrenders. The Sovereign commands. Man obeys. Human peace and fulfillment come through submission.

Parents are to be honored, kindness shown to slaves, the orphans and the widows protected, and charity dispensed to the poor. Honesty, patience, industry, honor, courage, and generosity will be rewarded at the last judgment; cruelty, dishonesty, greed, and selfishness punished. Heads of families are responsible for their kin and must treat all kindly and impartially. Requests for help must not be refused even if they seem unworthy.

The subjects of Allah govern as his representatives. They may not use force to convert "people of the Book"—Christians and Jews. They may fight in defense and may subjugate unbelievers (idolaters). "People of the Book" may not be drafted into military service. They can be assessed a levy for costs of the war.

Muhammed was anxious to expand his community beyond Medina. Victory over the idolaters in Mecca and possession of the holy Kaaba was his first goal. But those who had fled with him from Mecca years before were held back from attacking their kin by the ancient Arab concept of honor.

Month by month Muhammed kept reminding the impoverished refugees that they were suffering because of the merchants of Mecca. He finally raised a raiding party that intercepted a richly laden caravan bound for Mecca.

The Meccans learned in advance of the next attack on a caravan and sent extra soldiers. Muhammed's small army of three hundred was outnumbered three to one at the wells of Badr. Above the clashing swords and whistling arrows, the Prophet shouted, "All who die today will go at once to Paradise!" The Muslims routed the Meccans. Muhammed later reported that Allah had told him, "It was not ye who slew them. It was the One God."

The Mecca merchants sent a revenge force. This time Muhammed was hit in the face by a stone. A sword slammed against his helmet. He fell bleeding. Before the Meccans could finish him off, his friends grabbed him up and rushed him to safety.

Heartened by victory, the Meccans determined to rid

Arabia of the troublesome Muslims once and for all. They collected an army of twenty thousand and advanced on horses and camels towards Medina.

This time Muhammed had been forewarned. He had drilled his men in new techniques of warfare and had them dig a deep, wide trench along the side of the city where he expected the Meccans to attack.

Such defense against a military onslaught had never been used in Arabia. The Meccans were unable to get past the trench and had to lay siege to the city. Suddenly the Jews arose inside the city and attacked Muhammed's force from behind, forcing the Muslims toward their protective trench. Just in time, a desert storm descended on their Meccan enemies, forcing them to retreat to a shelter. Muhammed's troops then turned and decisively defeated the Jews and drove them out of Medina. The Battle of the Trench is the most celebrated victory in Islamic history.

News of Allah's "intervention" at the Battle of the Trench swept across Arabia. Tribal chieftains came to Muhammed pledging allegiance and promising that their people would submit to the will of Allah. Three Jewish tribes capitulated but declined to convert. Muhammed gave them treaties that guaranteed freedom of worship, self-government, and security so long as they paid the civil tax. The Meccan merchants were properly impressed and asked for a ten-year truce. They agreed to clear Mecca for three days a year so the Muslims could make their pilgrimage to the Kaaba in peace.

The peace was broken when a rump band of Meccans attacked one of Muhammed's tribal allies. The Muslims invaded Mecca and captured the city against only token opposition. When he reached the Kaaba, Muhammed rode around the sanctuary seven times, touching the Black

Stone with his rod each time. He thus made this ancient pagan ritual a part of Islam.

Muhammed enjoyed peace only two weeks. An allied army of thirty thousand idolaters advanced from the south. The Muslims met them outside Mecca and won another stunning victory. Holdout tribesmen were awed and converted by the thousands.

Muhammed took to the field once more, leading thirty thousand men toward a large settlement of Christian Arabs. He was met part way by the Christian prince who vowed allegiance but would not convert. Muhammed gave the Christians the same treaty he had given the Jews.

The Prophet was sixty-one now and weakening fast in Medina. He no longer slept with a different wife each night, but cohabited with only his favorite, Aishah. He sent his oldest and most trusted friend abu Bakr to Mecca as leader of the next pilgrimage. At the close of the pilgrimage, Muhammed's son-in-law Ali read a new revelation declaring that in the future no unbelievers would be allowed in the holy area.

Abu Bakr took over the leading of prayers. Early in July, 632, Muhammed came down with a fever. On Sunday, the 7th, he fell into a delirium. The next day he appeared better, then on Tuesday the fever rose rapidly. Near noon, his wife Aishah felt his hand go limp in her own. She heard only the soft whisper, "God forgive me, have compassion on me, and take me into the highest heaven." The Prophet of Islam was dead.

Muhammed's legacy was the Koran, the Islamic Bible. He was illiterate and had never written it down. But his faithful secretary, Zaid ibn Thabit, and others had kept notes on scraps of animal skins and bones.

The Koran is today the second most influential book in

the world, second only to the Bible. The leaders of Saudi Arabia, Libya, Tunisia, Morocco, and other Muslim theocracies rule by it. Arab soldiers carry metal-jacketed copies into war. Islam considers all science and true wisdom only a commentary on the sacred revelations to Muhammed.

The average Muslim reverences the Koran far more than the average Christian does the Bible. The Muslim is required to purify parts of his body before touching the holy book; if he has just had sexual intercourse, he must take a full bath.

There is an important difference between the Islamic doctrine of how the Koran was transmitted to Muhammed and how Christians believe the Bible was inspired. Muslims believe God "sent down" every word of the Koran exactly as he had written it in a preexistent book. The illiterate Prophet spoke exactly what he heard and the copiers preserved precisely what he said. Christians believe that the biblical authors were allowed to express their own personalities as they were inspired by the Holy Spirit.

The Koran differs from the Bible in other ways. It was presented through only one prophet. Over forty writers and editors were involved in writing the Bible. The Koran is much shorter. It contains only 114 surahs (chapters) which follow no chronological order. Most books of the Bible follow a time line.

To a considerable extent the Koran is based on the Bible, particularly the Pentateuch. Islam's book provides many parallels to biblical incidents, but often diverges from the biblical accounts. Muslims explain these differences as corrections by Allah of the biblical record. Christians hold they are merely apocryphal noninspired accounts.

The Koranic version of the life of Jesus is most interesting:

—Jesus was announced to Mary as "Messiah Jesus, an apostle to the Jews." As a sign to Mary that she would miraculously conceive the Messiah, God made the figure of a bird and breathed life into it.

—Mary gave birth under a palm beside a small stream.

—Jesus spoke from the cradle, "Verily I am the servant of God . . . a prophet." He followed in the "footsteps" of earlier Jewish prophets.

—The claim of Jesus' divinity was made by His followers who were ignorant of His true nature. Jesus would not have said He was God because He was a true prophet. Allah could have destroyed Jesus, had he chose.

—The Comforter (the Holy Spirit in John's Gospel) which Jesus promised was Muhammed. Just as the Old Testament foretold Jesus, so Jesus foretold Muhammed.

—The Jews did not kill Jesus, but only a man like Him. (Some Islamic authorities say God took the dead body of Jesus to Heaven while the Jews crucified a man who resembled Him. A Muslim tradition says the substitute was Simon of Cyrene who carried Jesus' cross. Another tradition holds that Jesus died and was buried in Kashmir. Still another tradition says Jesus will return to earth at the end of the world and slay the Antichrist, die, be buried beside Muhammed at Medina, then be resurrected from the dead alongside with Muhammed.)

The Koran vigorously denies that Jesus could have been divine:

"They say the Most Gracious has begotten a son! Indeed ye have put forth a thing most monstrous! For it is not compatible with the majesty of God that He should beget a son. Jesus Christ the son of Mary was no more than an apostle of God. . . . So believe in God and His

apostles. Say not Trinity. Desist. It will be better for you:
for God is One God."

Christian researchers in Islam are now taking a new
look at Muhammed and his times. Donald McCurry, a
missionary for eighteen years in Muslim Pakistan and
now on the faculty at Fuller Theological Seminary,
concludes that Muhammed "never had a chance to accept
Christ intelligently. He knew only the Christian heresies
of his time." Professor McCurry notes that the Christian
leader John of Damascus, who was born less than a
century after Muhammed, called Islam a Christian
heresy.

Dr. Arthur Glasser, dean of the School of Missions at
Fuller, concurs. "Muhammed saw [Christianity only] in
distortion. If he had known the real thing, he might have
become one of the great figures of church history. He was
still a reformer," Dean Glasser continues, "calling his
people back to the . . . God of Abraham. I think if we
Christians looked closer at Muhammed, we would find a
lot to admire. Until now we've concentrated on what we
don't like about him."

Adds David W. King, a Southern Baptist missionary to
Lebanon, "How different the history of the world might
have been if only Muhammed could have known the living
Christ!"

5

Why Are We Afraid
of Muslims?

In March, 1977, the movie *Mohammad, Messenger of God* opened in eleven U.S. theaters. It was produced by Moustapha Akkad, a Syrian-born American who raised $17 million from Arab sources to make English and Arabic versions of the story. Akkad had no actor portraying Muhammed because of a prohibition of Islam. Actors addressed an empty space where viewers were to imagine the Prophet standing.

A torrent of protests descended. Declared Grand Sheik Abdel Halim Mahmoud of Al Azhar University in Cairo, the most prestigious school of Islam in the world: "The Koran is revelation, and the life of the Prophet is a divine commentary on that revelation. The idea of them being portrayed by others is particularly offensive."

The announced showing of the film on Muhammed was the straw that broke the proverbial camel's back for

fifty-six-year-old Hamaas Abdul Khaalis, a former Seventh
Day Adventist and Catholic named Ernest McGhee who
had joined Elijah Muhammad's Nation of Islam ("Black
Muslims") in 1950 and was now leader of the breakaway
Hanafi Muslims. Four years before, Khaalis's home had
been violently invaded by seven men, five of whom were
later linked to the Black Muslims. The invaders brutally
murdered five of Khaalis's children, his nine-day-old
grandson, and a dedicated follower. Five of the invaders
were convicted of the murders, but given only moderate
sentences.

Islamic law decrees death-for-death vengeance. Khaalis
had been brooding over the leniency of the court ever
since. When he heard that the film on Muhammed was
about to be shown, something snapped. He decided to
execute justice by *jihad*—holy war.

About eleven the next morning Khaalis and six other
Hanafis burst into the Washington headquarters of B'nai
B'rith, the world's largest and oldest Jewish service
organization. Shouting that they were ready to die for
Allah, the Muslim fanatics herded dozens of hostages into
a conference room, shooting at some, slapping and
slashing at others.

Around noon three more Hanafis slipped into the
Islamic Center mosque on Embassy Row and hustled
eleven more hostages into a room. About two hours later
two more armed Hanafis shot their way into the District
of Columbia Building, just two blocks from the White
House. They killed a black radio newsman, wounded
three others, and took more hostages.

Khaalis made four demands: Hand over the Black
Muslims convicted for the 1973 murders. Have Wallace
Muhammed, leader of the Bilalians (the new name of the
Black Muslims), and boxer Muhammad Ali brought to

Washington. Give back $750 in legal fees resulting from a previous contempt of court citation against Khaalis. Ban the film on Muhammed because it was sacrilegious.

The movie was stopped and the $750 delivered to Khaalis. But authorities refused to surrender the prisoners, Wallace Muhammad, and Ali for fear the Hanafis would execute them all.

The Muslim ambassadors from Egypt, Iran, and Pakistan offered help. They read the Koran to Khaalis. The convincing passage was: "And let not the hatred of some people in shutting you out of the Sacred Mosque lead you into transgression and hostility on your part; help ye one another in righteousness and piety, but judge ye not one another in sin and rancor" (Surah 5:2-4). Khaalis gave up.

When the chilling thirty-eight-hour siege had ended—"the worst situation we've ever had," according to the FBI—it was learned that some of the Jewish hostages had been tortured. Also, the men and women had been separated by sex and the women made to cover their legs with newspapers. And a Christian clergyman was threatened with beheading after he began a theological argument.

Eleven months after the Hanafi terror in Washington, the *Reader's Digest* presented a report on another U.S. Muslim sect that was even more frightening. A select paramilitary group of Black Muslims, called the Fruit of Islam, had murdered scores, perhaps hundreds, of unrelated persons across the country for no other reason than that they were white. For killing four white "devils," a brother was to receive a button and a free trip "to the Holy City to see Brother Mohammed."

The American roots of the Black Muslims go back to the 1930s when W.D. Fard, an itinerant black preacher in Detroit syncretized cultic elements of Islam and

Christianity into a strange hybrid religion. Fard claimed that he had come from Mecca with this message from Allah: The first man created was black and the white and yellow races had developed through the genetic experiments of a black scientist named Yakub. Whites had been permitted to rule the world for six thousand years; their reign had ended in 1914 and the destruction of white civilization could come at any moment. When Fard died in 1934, his followers, who had taken on Islamic names, declared he had been an incarnation of Allah.

Elijah Muhammed, formerly Elijah Poole, another itinerant black preacher, took over as the "Divinely Inspired Messenger of Allah." Little happened until black nationalism flowered during the civil rights struggle of the fifties. Then blacks began joining by the thousands, pledging separatism from whites and abstinence from drugs, alcohol, ritually unclean foods, gambling, and illicit sex. The fiery, brilliant Malcolm X became Elijah Muhammed's right-hand man, displaying hatred for whites, and rejoicing over a hundred white Georgians killed in the crash of an Air France jet at Paris on June 3, 1962.

In 1964 Malcolm broke with Elijah Muhammed to form a rival organization. The following year he was assassinated. Two Black Muslims and another man were sentenced to life imprisonment for his murder.

The Black Muslims began bidding for respectability. They opened schools for ghetto black children, provided social services for inner-city blacks, developed black businesses without any government help, and started a two-hundred-bed hospital in Chicago. By 1973 they had "Temples of Islam" in seventy U.S. cities and claimed membership in the hundreds of thousands (an exaggeration, no doubt). Their most notable convert was the world heavyweight boxing champion Cassius Clay who took as his Islamic name Muhammad Ali.

Hamaas Abdul Khaalis and his group had already split from the larger group. The Hanafi's most publicized convert was the country's most famous black basketball player, Kareem Abdul-Jabbar. In 1973 Khaalis wrote to "ministers" in most Black Muslim temples, calling Elijah Muhammed a "lying deceiver." The murders in Khaalis's home came a few days later.

Elijah Muhammed died in 1975. His son Wallace Muhammed, who had been studying in Cairo, took the helm. The younger Muhammed led the group to drop the name Black Muslims "because true Islam is not racial," and take the title Bilalians in honor of Bilal, the first black convert to Islam. He also changed the name of their newspaper from *Muhammed Speaks* to *Bilalian News* and began crusading in print for an end to segregation and a revival of morality in America. Within months he received $26 million from oil-rich Arab nations to build a new showcase mosque in Chicago.

The notoriety of the Hanafis, the Fruit of Islam, and the former Black Muslims confirmed for many Westerners the belief that Islam is a religion that conquers and rules by the sword. Reports of plane hijackings and other violent actions by Palestinians helped add to this conviction. It is presumed by almost everyone in the West that Palestinians are Muslims, when in fact a large percentage have Christian backgrounds.

There have been other disquieting incidents. In the Philippines Muslim insurrectionists abducted two women members of the Wycliffe Bible Translators. They were later released without harm. However, two missionary nurses associated with Overseas Missionary Fellowship in Thailand were not. Margaret Morgan from Britain and

Minka Hanaskamp from Holland were taken by Muslim extremists who had been battling for annexation of southern Thai provinces to Muslim Malaysia where conversion of Muslims is a crime. The kidnappers demanded a half-million-dollar ransom from the mission and that letters be sent to the U.S. and British governments protesting Israeli injustices against Palestinians. Longstanding mission policy forbade the granting of either request. The nurses' skeletons were found later in the jungle. Each had been shot in the back of the head.

Added to such disturbing incidents are news dispatches pointing to Islamic missionary fervor throughout the world, including the traditionally Christian West. Items:

—The influential American evangelical monthly, *Eternity*, headlined in 1978: "The Muslims Are Coming . . . Is That a Mosque in Your Neighborhood?" The writer described how Arab petrodollars were advancing Islam and suggested "there may be two million Muslims on the North American continent."

—Islamic books, magazines, and newspapers are now in most libraries and sold in drugstores, newsstands, and on street corners. One book is titled, *Islam—the Religion of the Future*. One periodical boasts a circulation of 740,000. A recurring theme is that Christianity has failed, Christian America is corrupt, and only Islam has the remedy to redeem America.

—Oil-rich Libya is said to be levying a special 4 per cent tax to promote Islam, particularly in North America and Africa. The money helps pay for Islamic centers, schools, mosques (such as the Bilalian showcase in Chicago), and Muslim lecturers.

—Thirteen hundred Americans made *hadj* (pilgrimage)

to Mecca last year. Among them were a well-known American TV reporter and a bureau chief for a major U.S. network. Both are stationed in Saudi Arabia and recent converts to Islam. The bureau chief is a former New York Jew.

—Islam is growing in Great Britain at a rate of 10.8 per cent annually, while church attendance continues to plummet (only 18 per cent of the English were going to church in 1978). According to the *Eternity* article, there will soon be over three hundred mosques to accommodate Muslim growth. In April of 1977 the festival of Islam was opened by Queen Elizabeth and attended by thousands.

The Evangelical Alliance Mission reported in 1978 that a newspaper published in Mecca recently headlined: "Britain ripe for conversions to Islam." The writer reported, "It is common now to see English Muslims going back and forth to pray in the mosques. . . . It is so precious to see English people standing facing Mecca in reverence and meditation."

—Islam has become the second largest religion in France, although Roman Catholicism continues to claim the great majority of French citizenry. Islam is also advancing in Italy where the late King Faisal of Saudi Arabia gave seven million dollars to build a mosque in Rome.

—The Arab Authority for Agricultural Investment and Development plans to spend six billion dollars in the African Sudan (now 70 per cent Muslim; 25 per cent pagan animist; and only 5 per cent Christian) over the next twenty to twenty-five years. Super-wealthy Kuwait is providing 500 million dollars to develop the Senegal River basin in West Africa. The United Arab Emirates are now spending over 30 per cent of their annual income on foreign aid. Carps a Christian missionary: "Islam is making oil Muslims."

—In an article on holy war, *Time* said, "Most of the religious struggles around the world involve Muslims. . . . Such conflicts may be an expression of a resurgent Islam." *Time* quoted Duke University political scientist Ralph Braibanti: "This may be the moment in history when money, diplomacy and strategy join together in providing a new content for the renaissance of Islamic identity and perhaps of Islam itself."

—Population statistics show Muslim wives bearing children at four times the rate Christian and Jewish women are giving birth. Thirteen of the fifteen nations with the highest fertility rates are either Islamic kingdoms or majority Muslims. The ten lowest nations are all predominantly Christian. Israel's birth rate is less than half of Saudi Arabia's and some other Muslim countries. The population imbalance between Arabs and Jews in Israel is widening at a pace alarming to the Israeli government. If the present scale continues, Arabs inside Israel will be able to outvote Jews by the year 2000.

—Most ominous are fears that Arab feelings toward Israel flow from the concept of *jihad* (holy war). Many Israelis have said this, but there have also been confirmations from some Muslim Arabs. Egypt's Grand Sheik Abdel Halim Mahmoud called the "Yom Kippur" war of 1973 against Israel a holy war. "We are fighting as the early Muslims fought against the infidels," he shouted in Cairo's Al Azhar mosque. "All the dead in battle are sure of paradise. . . . If all Muslims did their duty and took a weapon, there would be no problem." Sheik Mahmoud and other Islamic authorities in Egypt also went on radio and boosted troop morale by comparing the battles of Muhammed with the fight against the Israelis. During this same war the Saudi Arabian Minister of the

Interior urged his fellow Muslims to "destroy the enemies of religion [Islam]."

All of this adds fire to the Middle East conflict. The struggle between the Arabs and Israelis takes on a broader and more alarming connotation to Christians and Jews elsewhere. Many have visions of Islam being spread over the world by a gigantic spill of Arab oil money. Some visualize Muslim armies, equipped with nuclear weapons, conquering in the name of Allah.

Wild imaginations? Whether so or not, many non-Muslims are frightened of Islam and its oil power. Their concerns must be addressed, not by denials, but by hard exploration into Islam's history and present purposes.

What is meant by *jihad* (holy war)? Is it propagandizing and persuasion of beliefs in democratic ways? Does it call for economic pressure, even violent force, when peaceful missionary strategy fails? Is Islam united in methods and goals? Or is it divided between those who would strive for an allied Islamic kingdom and those who prefer democratic secular states, where freedom to worship and propagate one's faith is written into the constitution?

The answers to these questions are rooted in Islamic history during the first century after Muhammed.

Muhammed did not invent holy war. The practice is as old as mankind. The Jews of Joshua's day fought against *herem*—idolatrous worship of the pagan peoples in Canaan that included sexual orgies and child sacrifice. They were commanded to stamp out completely the contagion of those possessed by *herem*. Not even the Canaanite children were exempt from the sword.

The Old Testament Hebrews soon turned sacred conquest to selfish ends. They lost the idealism of fighting for a moral and spiritual kingdom in which peace, justice, and righteousness would reign. They battled for privilege and profit. They became materialistic and greedy and enamored with worldly power. After independence was taken from them and they became a vassal of foreign powers, they dreamed of the restoration of past glories. Their messianic thinking was mired in such selfish chauvinism. When Jesus came, they could not comprehend a universal spiritual kingdom without nationality and based on equality and justice for all.

In Muhammed's early revelations, the Arabic word *jihad* meant only "struggle" or "striving" for Allah's cause, including a life of good deeds. Then it was broadened to envelop a doctrine of self-defense. "Fight against those who fight against you. But begin not hostilities. Allah loves not aggressors."

Muhammed's first battles were essentially defensive and necessary to Islam's survival. The argument, as later put down in the Koran, was that war is preferable to peace, until Islam is secure.

A later pronouncement extended *jihad* to attack. Muhammed's truce with the pagan tribes around Mecca gave them four months to return home. If they did not then become Muslims, they would be liable to attack.

Muslims could fight Jews and Christians until they bowed to Islamic rule and agreed to pay a tax for security and freedom of worship. But pressure could also be put on Jews to convert. One Koranic revelation addressed to Jews declared: "O ye to whom the Scriptures have been given! Believe in what we have sent down confirmatory of the Scripture which is in your hands, ere we efface your features, and twist your head round backward, or curse you as we cursed the sabbath breakers (idolaters). . . . If the people of the Book believe and have the fear of God," it was promised, "we will surely put away their sins from

them, and will bring them into the gardens of delight
. . ." (Koran, Surah 4:50, 70). Some Islamic scholars
today say this passage was aimed at the Jews in Medina
who gave Muhammed so much trouble, and that it should
not literally be followed today.

The unity of Islam is no less a fiction than the
organizational unity of Christianity or Judaism. The first
cracks in the system began appearing after Muhammed
died. He had not provided for a *caliph* (successor), and on
the day of his death there was great confusion among his
relatives and close friends at Medina. They argued
passionately about who would be their new leader, while
their Prophet's body lay alone in the hut of his favorite
wife, Aishah. Not until the following day did they bury
him under the floor of the hut.

The problem was that there was no direct male heir.
None of Muhammed's wives had borne him a son.

The Prophet's closest male relative was Ali, his cousin
and the son of the uncle, abu Talib, who had taken the boy
Muhammed into his household. Ali was also married to
Fatima, Muhammed's daughter by a lesser-ranking wife.
Ali claimed the caliphate on the basis of this double
kinship.

Muhammed's favorite wife Aishah opposed Ali,
perhaps because of jealousy. She was supported by the
Muhajirun, the circle of the Prophet's oldest followers.
They presented abu Bakr, father of another of the
Prophet's wives, as the first caliph. Ali and his supporters
grudgingly conceded. They likely anticipated that abu
Bakr would not live long.

Abu Bakr, the first caliph of Islam, did live only two
years. But he was no caretaker successor. He spent the
first year quelling rebellions against the rule of
Muhammed's Muslim converts in Medina. Then he looked

beyond the borders of Arabia.

It was a propitious time for a dynamic new power that combined religious fervor and political loyalties. The great empires of east and west, Persian and Byzantine, were weak from fighting each other and from putting down rebellions. The churches in the Byzantine territories were nationalistic and resented the string-pulling by the emperor's hand-picked prelates.

The caliph sent one Muslim army into southern Babylonia, then controlled by Persia, and another west into Byzantine Syria. Syria then covered the entire length of ancient Canaan, from Egypt in the south and past present Lebanon in the north. Both thrusts were successful.

The western army pursued a Byzantine force to the gates of Damascus. After a six-month siege the Byzantine soldiers surrendered. The Muslims entered the old city to the cheers of the Christian and Jewish population. They were tired of sheltering foreign soldiers and paying war debts incurred by the Christian Byzantine emperor at Constantinople. They gratefully accepted the proclamation by General Khalid ibn al-Walid, who spoke as Caliph abu Bakr's personal representative:

> In the name of Allah, the Compassionate, the Merciful. . . . To the people of Damascus . . . safety for themselves, their property, their churches, and the walls of their city . . . as long as they pay the *jizya* ["tribute tax"].

Later the Christians and Jews discovered a number of "catch 22s" in Muslim rule. A synagogue or church could not be built without permission. A Jewish or Christian congregation could not take over an abandoned mosque.

But Muslims could change a house of worship formerly used by Christians and Jews into a mosque. The Muslims built in Damascus their famous Omayyad Mosque on the site of three successive sanctuaries, an Aramaean temple to fertility deities, a Roman temple to mythical Jupiter, and a Christian cathedral.

Also, religious freedom under Islam meant that Christians and Jews could only practice their own religions within their communities. They could not proselytize Muslims, nor could Muslims convert. Muslims were expected to evangelize their neighbors, and many professing Christians and Jews did find it advantageous to acknowledge Allah as the One God and Muhammed his apostle.

There were other reminders that Islam was the final word from God. For instance, no Christian or Jew could build a house higher than the residences of his Muslim neighbors.

From Damascus the Muslim army pushed south into the Jordan River valley and camped on a tributary stream known as the Yarmuk. A pursuing Byzantine force of fifty thousand caught up with the audacious Arabians there.

The Byzantine soldiers were conscripts. Half were from Christian Armenia, long at odds with church authorities in Constantinople. Fearful of mutiny, the Byzantine general ordered his soldiers chained together, ten on a shackle, thirty ranks deep.

With swords flashing, and shouting "Allahu akbar! God is greater!" the Muslims plunged into battle. They almost annihilated the demoralized Byzantines.

Caliph abu Bakr did not live to enjoy the sweets of that victory. He died in July 634. The Muhajirun circle of elders quickly met and by consensus named Omar, another old friend of Muhammed, to be the next caliph.

Caliph Omar is one of the noblest figures in Islamic history. He had the moral standards of Isaiah, the concern for the poor of Amos, the military sagacity of Judas Maccabaeus, the missionary zeal of the apostle Paul, and the tolerance of Barnabas. He was said to have owned only one shirt and mantle which his wife could never keep patched. He reportedly walked the streets of Medina at night to see that everyone was well fed and housed. He continually reminded his administrators that the community treasury belonged to the people and not to the government.

The year after his appointment, Omar's generals conquered the rest of Babylonia and Syria. The caliph himself joined a pilgrimage to Jerusalem. Nearing the Holy City, he dismounted from his camel and entered on foot in reverence to the holy places.

The Byzantine Christian patriarch welcomed him and escorted him into the Church of the Holy Sepulcher. It was at one of the times of Muslim prayer, and a soldier started to spread the caliph's prayer mat on the floor. Omar softly declined and stepped outside the sanctuary for his devotions. He feared that if he prayed here some of his people might build a mosque on the spot and destroy the historic church.

Omar gave the patriarch of Jerusalem a treaty which is cherished by tolerant Muslims today:

> In the name of Allah, the Merciful, the Compassionate. This is the covenant which Omar ibn al-Khattab, the servant of Allah, the Commander of the Faithful, grants to the people of Allah, the Holy House. He grants them security of their lives, their possessions, their churches and crosses . . . they shall have

freedom of religion and none shall be molested
unless they rise up in a body . . . they shall pay a
tax instead of military service . . . and those who
leave the city shall be safeguarded until they
reach their destination. . . .

While in Jerusalem, Omar asked to be taken to the
summit of Mt. Moriah. A Jewish tradition says that this
was the biblical mount on which Abraham prepared to
offer Isaac as a sacrifice. A Muslim tradition claims the
beloved son was Ishmael. Here three successive Jewish
temples had been built. From here also Muhammed was
supposed to have made his nocturnal ascension to heaven
and back. This was the reason for Omar's visit.

The patriarch led the Muslim caliph to a crumbling
stone platform that was covered with debris. Omar stood
and meditated for a few moments. Then he reportedly
cleared the refuse away and instructed his men that the
site should be reconsecrated as a holy place. Later (691)
the octagonal Mosque of Omar, better known as the Dome
of the Rock, was constructed on the summit amidst a
thirty-four-acre compound which contained other Muslim
holy places. The Dome is today the third holiest shrine of
Islam, behind only Medina and Mecca.

Islam marched on. Persian Mesopotamia, the ancestral
home of Abraham which includes today much of Iran, fell
next. The Persians were in full retreat. The great empire
had dominated much of the Middle East for over twelve
hundred years, except for a short period during the fourth
century when Alexander the Great held sway, and
boasted of such illustrious rulers as Cyrus and Darius I.
Now it was crumbling before the expansion of Islam.

Egypt, the center of Coptic Christianity, was taken
from the Byzantine power. The Copts had resented the

heavy-handed effort of the Byzantine emperor Heraclius in trying to bring them back under the authority of the Catholic Church. They had chafed at high Byzantine taxes. They welcomed the new Muslim rulers as the Christians in Damascus had done. The Muslims, in turn, gave the Copts the usual treaty. They replaced only the Byzantine administrators and left Copt officials at their posts.

Byzantine troops were now falling back across North Africa. The Muslim soldiers that had conquered Egypt joined the native Berber peoples in their revolt against the Byzantines. Within a short time the Berbers were converted and the wide sweep of the Sahara and other lands that make up present Libya, Tunisia, Algeria, and Morocco belonged to Islam. Many of the oldest Christian sanctuaries in the world were made into mosques.

In less than a generation the advance forces of Islam had acquired one of the greatest empires in history. In another century Islamic rule would stretch from Spain to India. The subjects of Allah would subsequently spread their religion to some of the Pacific islands, long before the arrival of European voyagers and the first Christian missionaries.

How did Islam move so far and so fast? A Protestant missionary leader of the early twentieth century credits Islam's advance with the new religion's "easy-going character and low moral standards, propelled by the power of the sword and of fanaticism."

One need not be a Muslim to disagree. Muhammed united the tribes of Arabia that had hitherto spent their energies in fighting one another and in idolatrous debauchery. The new religion brought discipline, morality, and purpose. Too much has been made of harems, which some Muslim rulers later adopted from

Persia, and Muslim exploitation of women. Muslims were more like the stern Puritans of colonial America than the stereotypes of modern movies and novels.

This is only one side of the story. Persia and Byzantium, the two great empires which Islam confronted, were in decline. The Byzantine Catholic church and state system of the seventh century were generally corrupt. Religious life had continued to degenerate. There was little spiritual power in churches which had been founded by the vanguard of the first-century church. Institutional Christianity had become gummed with ritualistic claptrap and a priestly hierarchy that elevated clergy above laity and bred pride and envy.

Early Islamic practices were actually more like those of first-century Christianity than were Byzantine practices. Islam had no priesthood. Anyone could officiate at the Friday service. Prayers were simple and related to daily life. If no mosque was available, the faithful could gather for prayers, reading of the Koran, and a sermon in a home or a public building.

This was Islam in its morning of glory and greatness. In later times it fragmented into sects and schools, which to varying degrees became encrusted with layers of traditions and superstitions. Today there are almost as many brands of Islam as Christianity. Some are as bizarre to Islamic scholars as the Appalachian snake handlers are to Christian theologians.

Seeds of disunity in a movement or institution germinate in struggles between young and old, liberals and conservatives, and personalities who attract followings. Such struggles are inevitable where humans associate in common cause. Division usually comes in the generations immediately following the death of a dynamic leader.

Such was the case with Islam. The old men had gotten their way with the first two caliphs, abu Bakr and Omar. Ali, their chief opponent, was young and could wait.

The infighting began in 644 after the beloved Omar was stabbed by a Persian war captive while leading early morning prayers. After he died, it was disclosed that he had made no provision for a successor.

Ali and Othman, another of Muhammed's sons-in-law, through a political marriage, and three from the old council met as a board of election. The old men still could not stomach Ali, but they were willing to compromise on Othman. He was probably the least qualified of the group.

Othman was from the clan of Umayyah. He immediately angered other clans by appointing his kinsmen to the important governorships in conquered territories.

The new caliph of Islam stirred up more trouble when he sought to establish an official Koran from versions that had been written down after Muhammed's death. He appointed the Prophet's old scribe and three other men to put together an "authorized version." When they completed their work, he ordered all other versions destroyed. Copies of the authorized edition were then sent to mosques in every major city of the empire.

Aishah, the Prophet's favorite spouse, was still living and revered as "Mother of the Believers." She and the old men led a tumultuous protest. It was bad enough, they said, that the new caliph had put his relatives in office. It was unforgivable that he should make his own falsified and incomplete version of the Koran and destroy all others. Certain embarrassing revelations to Muhammed which condemned Othman's relatives, they charged, had been suppressed.

The former Muslim governor of Egypt, who Othman

had deposed in favor of a kinsman, brought a small army to the protest in Medina. Caliph Othman quickly promised reforms.

Hardly had the ex-governor left when the caliph's alarmed relatives descended. Fearful of losing their jobs, they persuaded Othman to announce in the Medina mosque that the ex-governor had seen himself in the wrong and left. This flip-flop angered other Medinese. They stoned Othman into unconsciousness on the floor of the mosque.

The ex-governor and his loyalists came back. A supporter of Othman threw a stone and killed one. The rebels stormed the caliph's house and killed him.

Ali stepped forth and claimed the caliphate. Protected by a bodyguard, he moved the office to Baghdad where he had a large following.

The intrigue became more complicated. Muawiyah, governor of Syria, was next of kin to the slain caliph and honor bound to avenge his death. He demanded that Ali hand over Othman's murderers. Ali wouldn't or couldn't produce them.

Muawiyah sent troops to Baghdad—reportedly armed with copies of the official Koran fixed to the points of their lances—to force Ali to comply. Ali ordered his troops to fight.

Ali won this battle but lost the war. The balance of power swung to Muawiyah. Ali was assassinated in a mosque on January 24, 661 by three members of the Islamic Kharijite sect. Muawiyah claimed the leadership.

Ali's first son, Hassan, now declared himself caliph on the basis that he was the Prophet's grandson. Then he resigned in exchange for a large sum of money.

Muawiyah died and was succeeded by his son Yazid. Ali's second son, Hussein, contested Yazid for the caliphate.

Yazid sent soldiers to force Hussein to renounce his claim. In a battle Hussein was killed. His supporters promptly acclaimed him a martyr.

From this split between contenders for the caliphate came the two major factions or schools which exist today in world Islam, Shiites, and Sunnites.

Shiites represent about 15 per cent of Islam. They hold to the straight kinship line of successors to Muhammed, and reject all appointed caliphs as frauds. Every year they present an annual passion play to commemorate the martyr Hussein's death.

Shiites acknowledge Ali as the first *imam*, meaning "recognized leader." They prefer this title to caliph. After Ali, they recognize only Hassan, Hussein, and nine other hereditary heirs. They believe that the twelfth *imam* remains hidden. He is the Muslim Mahdi ("spiritual leader") who will appear at the end of the world and restore rightful leadership to Islam.

The Shiites also say that Allah's revelations did not end with Muhammed. Allah, they hold, gave more truth to the eleven *imams* who followed Muhammed. These and the hidden twelfth *imam* are infallible and sinless.

Shiites have splintered into many sects. Each claims possession of a special mystical revelation received by one of the *imam*'s. The largest Shiite sect is the Sufis. The Sufis worship in stillness, much like Quakers, and seek the immediate presence of God.

The most militant Shiite sect is the Ahmadiya. They claim the nineteenth century Hazrat Mirza Ghulam as the hidden *imam*. They quote a prophecy that predicts their sect will one day be internationally accepted. They already have eleven thousand followers in England. Adherents must give 16 per cent of their income for missionary work.

76

Druzes are the most extreme Shiite variant. They guard their rites with extreme secrecy. They claim that the sixth descendant of Muhammed in the Shiite kinship line was the hidden *imam*. He was God incarnate and has never died. He remains hidden and will reveal himself at the day of judgment. Some Druzes live on the Golan Heights where families are divided by the military border between Syria and Israel. Relatives can only cry out to one another across the guarded boundary.

Sunnites ("path followers") reject kinship succession and accept the historical caliphs. They hold that divine revelation ceased at the death of Muhammed. Among the Sunnites an *imam* is only the leader of mosque prayers.

For both Sunnites and Shiites the Koran is the highest authority, although many Shiites still claim that the holy book was corrupted by Caliph Othman.

The second authority for Sunnites is the tradition of Muhammed. God's choice of Muhammed as his final messenger, they say, gave the Prophet such authority that *everything* about him is important. Consequently they have collected the writings of the companions of Muhammed on everything the Prophet said and did. This material includes enormous details. For example, there are prayers for entering and leaving a house, going and coming from the bathroom, retiring and rising, visiting the sick, and passing a cemetery.

One of the most interesting traditions held among both Shiites and Sunnites concerns the Day of Judgment. They say that all the prophets from Adam to Jesus will be there. As each person appears, the prophets will transfer the role of intercessor, each to the other, until all have disclaimed the privilege. Then Muhammed will step up and intercede with God. He will do this for each person until only the most pernicious are left in Hell. For them not even Muhammed's intercession can avail.

Sunnites have two other regulative sources of law, both based on the traditions and the Koran.

The first is *kiyas* or analogy. The Koran prohibits the use of wine. By analogy should other intoxicants be forbidden? The Koran condemns the eating of pork. Is horse meat also unclean?

The second is *Ijma'* or consensus. This is based on one of the most important sayings attributed to Muhammed, "My community will never agree in error." Every Sunnite knows that a belief held by the greater part of Islam in history is infallibly true. It is this idea of consensus that keeps Sunnites on a stretch band between past and present. The belief in consensus is so strong that many Arab Sunnites prefer to discuss an issue until a majority has reached a consensus on a solution rather than take a vote as Westerners would do.

Sunnite Islam can be immensely complicated. There are four different systems for interpreting the law!

By temperament, Sunnites are more inclined to be rationalistic and legalistic than Shiites. Sunnites are celebrated hair-splitters, but they are more pragmatic than philosophic. The interpretation must be grounded in reality.

Sunnism has also proliferated into numerous sects. They vary from extreme liberals to fanatical extremists. Anwar Sadat and Colonel Muammar el Qaddafi, presidents of Egypt and Libya respectively, for example, are both Sunnites. Yet there is an infinity of differences between them.

Qaddafi and small group of junior officers overthrew Libya's conservative King Idris in 1969. He has since turned Libya into a puritanical Islamic kingdom and has waged holy war against the foreign Christian community.

He has closed down most Christian churches, including the Protestant Union Church of Tripoli which was attended mostly by American oil and diplomatic families. He charged the Union Church with publishing literature about "Israelis." The literature was Sunday school stories about Old Testament characters.

His animosity against the United States is exceeded only by his hatred for Israel. He is believed to use Libyan oil money in supporting anti-Western terrorism in many countries. His admitted rule of thumb for foreign aid is: "Will it hurt Israel? Will it help Islam?"

Yet Qaddafi lives austerely in two sparsely furnished rooms with his wife and zealously keeps tabs on the social needs of his people. He has been known to disguise himself and prowl the streets of Tripoli, looking for people in need, and checking on how poor Libyans are treated by public officials.

Sadat is friendly and tolerant toward foreigners and people of other faiths. Kissinger, a Jew, is "my friend Henry." Cyrus Vance, the present American Secretary of State, is "my dear friend, Cy." The U.S. president is "my dear Brother Carter." He can even speak kindly of Israeli leaders and enjoys a delightful rapport with Golda Meir.

In private worship Sadat is no less devout than his neighbor Qaddafi. He is always at Friday mosque services and keeps the "duties" of Islam faithfully. Also a mystic, Sadat speaks of having an "experience" with God when imprisoned in solitary confinement during the corrupt regime of King Farouk.

Sadat will have no truck with Muslim extremists. He remembers the fanatical Muslim Brotherhood which murdered Egyptian Prime Minister Mahmud Fahmy Nokrashy in 1949 and the "Black Saturday" burning of Cairo in 1952 by members of the group.

One of his own cabinet ministers, Sheikh Mohammed Zahabi, was killed by a sect known as the Society of Imprecation and Flight From Sin. Zahabi had been an outspoken critic of the sect which advocated the overthrow of Egypt's tolerant government and replacement by an Islamic state governed strictly under the Koran. During recent peace negotiations with Israel, the five sect members were brought to trial and hanged for the kidnap-murder.

The whole Arab Muslim Middle East is a jumble of sects, divisions, and parties within Islam. Every country is different and full of contradictions that defy generalizations. Saudi Arabia, for instance, is politically pro-Western, but enforces the Koranic law with a passion on both citizens and noncitizens alike. In 1978 a princess and her lover were executed for committing adultery. Shortly afterwards two Britishers were each flogged for having made beer, a violation of Saudi Arabian laws.

There is no centralized religious hierarchy or headquarters in Islam such as Catholics have in the Vatican. There is no agreement on holy war and how it should be waged. There is only a loosely defined loyalty to the community and program of Islam, a profound reverence for Allah's messenger Muhammed and other great leaders of Islam, as well as the holy places in Mecca, Medina, and Jerusalem and for the sacred Koran.

6

What Have Arabs Given
to the World Besides Oil?

During the terrible American winter of 1976-77 an easterner, whose town had run out of sand for its icy streets, wrote the *Washington Star-News:* "It seems the Arabs have everything we want, first oil, now sand."

Oil and big spenders, sand and camels, propaganda and terrorism—these are about the extent of what many Westerners think the Arabs have given the world.

Some have looked a little further and grudgingly admit that Arabs are getting educated. They note, for example, that Egyptian ambassador Ashraf Ghorbal, who helped talk the Washington Hanafis into giving up, has a master's degree and doctorate from Harvard. And that Sheik Ahmed Zaki al-Yamani, Saudi Arabia's Minister of Petroleum and Mineral Resources and the most powerful oil magnate on earth, studied psychiatry at Columbia University and international corporate law at Harvard

Law School. And that three thousand Saudis are now studying in U.S. schools under grants from their government.

That's because the Saudis can afford it, people say. But look at the Palestinians. They're just poor farmers, sheep herders, tourist guides, and street corner peddlers waiting for a chance to sneak aboard a Western airliner with a grenade. Indeed, look at the Palestinians. They now have the highest literacy rate in the Middle East. Sixty-four thousand Palestinians earned university degrees between 1948 and 1967. That's only three thousand less than the number of Israeli graduates (from a higher population) during the same period.

The apologists won't give up. "Most educated Arabs studied in the West or at schools started by Westerners in the Middle East," they say. True. And for the Saudis and other oil-rich Arabs: "Western technology developed their oil and made it possible for them to buy the educational and cultural advantages from us."

Such patronizing and prejudicial attitudes have been cultivated in Western public and religious education. An early twentieth-century Protestant text on the Islamic world is typical: "In most Mohammedan countries, the general ignorance of the people is plainly evident in the rude and crude methods of argiculture, building and transportation. . . . The first pump ever seen in eastern Arabia was imported by the missionaries, and in Oman many children still use the bleached shoulder-blades of camels instead of slates at school. . . .

". . . There is no power of reform from within. Falsehood, immorality, slavery, the degradation of marriage, the pollution of the home, the crushing yoke of universal ignorance and superstition—all these [in the Muslim world] can be uprooted and destroyed only by

Him who is the Way, the Truth, and the Life, the Light of the world and the Savior of men."

More recently, a fund raiser for the United Jewish Appeal told a Jewish Welfare Federation meeting in Chattanooga: "We [Jews] pay our due respect to parents and grandparents. Compare this to Muslim treatment of the elderly, which generally means turning old people out on the streets to beg."

Among most Protestant evangelicals, Arab "backwardness" is attributed to a supposed curse on Arabs for persecuting Jews. A 1976 picture-and-text tract published for sale to Protestant missions is one example. After describing the glory of Egyptian rulers of Joseph's time who treated Jews well, the tract concludes: "Today, Egyptian tourist guides can only boast about her glorious past. Egypt is now a backward nation, full of memories, relying on others for aid. . . . Egypt is still the enemy of Israel."

Of course there is poverty and backwardness in Egypt and other predominantly Muslim countries. But similar social conditions exist in many other lands, including "Christian" Latin America and even in some parts of the United States.

Such illustrations reflect Western ignorance of Arab accomplishments. The ignorance comes from having been taught the European view of history which has practically blanked out almost five hundred years of Arab greatness when Europe was languishing in the medieval Dark Ages.

Western affluence and cultural greatness is credited to the inventiveness of European scholars and the knowledge they gleaned from the Greeks and other ancient civilizations, while the contributions of Arabs have been passed over. The truth is that without Arab inventiveness and Arab translation of scientific and philosophical works from the Greeks and other ancient civilizations during Islam's "Golden Age," we would likely still be riding buggies instead of jet planes. Space flights and computers would be a hundred years in the future. Says Dr. Warren Webster, president of the Conservative Baptist Foreign Mission Society, a former missionary to Muslims and a respected authority on the Muslim world: "We might as well admit it: our Renaissance in the West goes back to the Golden Age of the Arabs."

To understand what happened we must return to the eighth century. The political structure of the western Roman Empire had broken up. The Roman Catholic church was tightening control over its subjects and baptizing pagans by the thousands. The papacy gained secular authority. In areas where anarchy often threatened to stamp out all order, it preserved certain basics of civilized life and lessened the influence of barbaric, pagan practices among many European tribes. Learning, however, was usually relegated to the monastics who preserved many literary treasures, including the Bible, but remained generally isolated from the common people.

However, religious dissenters were dealt with harshly. "Heretics," daring to challenge any dogma, were put to death or sent into exile. Jews in Spain were lined up before baptismal fonts and ordered to submit or die. Jews elsewhere were drafted into the middle class where they served as a buffer between wealthy nobles and the peasant masses.

While this was happening in Europe, the Muslim Arabs kept extending their empire. Having carried the Koran across North Africa, Islam's General Musa dispatched in 711 a Berber officer named Taria with seven thousand soldiers across the straits that divided Africa from

Europe. They crossed at the foot of a rock mountain, which became known as Jebel Tariq ("Tariq's Mountain," later corrupted into Gibraltar). The Muslim thrust was intended only as a pirate excursion. But after winning an easy victory over twelve thousand Visigoths, they rolled across Spain and crossed the Pyrenees into France. The caliph, then at Damascus, was reportedly angered that the Muslims had crossed the sea. But he apparently did nothing to reverse the conquest. The Muslims held southern France for twenty years before being driven back into Spain by Charles Martel's forces at the historic Battle of Tours. Had Martel lost and the Berber Arabs moved on across Europe, America might have been colonized by Muslims. Instead, the Berber Arabs were content to occupy Spain where they became known as Moors. They were also called "Veil Wearers" because of the Berber custom of men going veiled.

After the conquest of Spain, the Muslim Omayyad dynasty of caliphs at Damascus sought to consolidate the Islamic Empire and convert the millions of people they had conquered. In 747 the powerful Abbasid family, lineal descendants of an uncle of Muhammed, overthrew the Omayyads and moved the caliphal capital to Baghdad.

After the coup an Abassid general invited eighty members of the losing family to a peace dinner. Once inside the hall, executioners sprang from hiding and murdered every guest. The executioners then went after the grandson of the former caliph who had not attended the feast. Forewarned, he jumped into the Euphrates River and swam to the other side. He escaped to Spain and set up a rival capital at Cordoba that lasted almost three hundred years.

Then in the year 909 a powerful Shiite family, claiming direct descent from Muhammed, broke away from the

Baghdad caliphate. From Cairo they ruled Palestine and North Africa until A.D. 1171, while the Baghdad caliphs controlled the rest of the Middle East.

Even with three political divisions, the Muslim Arabs maintained a unity of spirit within Islam. They could be bitter political enemies, but as servants of Allah they were brothers.

During this time, Europe, excluding Muslim Spain, settled into feudalism. Unknown to Europeans, the Arab world made incredible advances in astronomy, mathematics, chemistry, medicine, agriculture, engineering, linguistics, art, literature and other fields that were unequalled before that time.

Why did this flowering of genius occur in Islam instead of Catholic Europe?

For two important reasons: (1) Catholicism discouraged secular learning, considered most science of little value and opposed views which conflicted with church tradition, while Islam rewarded the accomplishment of its scholars and scientists. (2) Catholicism shackled its best minds while Islam welcomed and protected Christian and Jewish scholars, considered heretics in the West, and allowed them to work.

Catholicism had inherited the dualism of spirit and matter that seduced much of Christendom in the third and fourth centuries. The papacy said the church taught all man needed to know, so there was little need in studying the physical world. Desires of the flesh were evil, especially sexual desire, most ecclesiastics declared; the highest calling was to renounce the flesh and cultivate the spirit. Thus came the separation of clergy and laity, a celibate priesthood, and monasticism where the divinity of Christ was empahsized to the exclusion of His humanity.

Christians in the Arab world were in some ways closer to Islam. They exalted the humanity of Christ to extremes. They were not inclined to be monastic. Their spiritual leaders could marry and enjoy a normal family life. They believed that the physical world, within limits, was to be understood and enjoyed.

Christians, Muslims, and Jews in the Middle East were all closer to their common Judaistic heritage. They agreed that the world was one, that the material universe was the visible "cloak of God," that the universe was not static, as Europeans tended to think, but dynamic and expanding. Creation was continuing and there could be no conflict between astronomy and theology or mathematics and theology. Science was an affirmation of faith, not the enemy of true belief. And Islam said that above all else the physical world must be brought into submission to God and the service of His people.

Islam was not rooted in a "chosen people," but in converts from scattered tribes. They had developed strong clan loyalties. They knew the rudiments of farming and sheepherding and trading. But they had not developed a great culture as had the Babylonians, Hebrews, Persians, and Greeks.

So it was natural for the Muslim Arabs to begin mining the knowledge of past civilizations, especially Greek. Fortunately the Greeks had left their wisdom in manuscripts. In Europe the priceless writings lay hidden in the dust of monasteries, unintelligible to most monks. However, some Nestorian monks realized their value. Refugees from Byzantine Catholicism, they gathered up bundles of precious Greek writings and fled to Persia. Arab scholars helped them translate the ancient wisdom of Greece into Arabic.

Much of the translation was done at the great Baghdad House of Wisdom, founded by Caliph Mamoun in A.D. 803. For approximately three centuries this was the world's greatest center of learning. Whole schools of linguist-translators and other scholars developed here.

Mamoun put a great Nestorian Christian scholar, Hynanyn ibn Ishaq, at the head of this academy. Hynanyn employed the greatest Christian, Jewish, and Muslim minds of that day.

The Arab researchers (a term used to denote all the scholars who used the Arabic language and worked within Arab culture) at Baghdad went first to the Greek philosophers to discover and develop rationales for religious truths. The Sunnite Muslims in power at Baghdad made much of the Islamic doctrine of consensus. Agreement constituted truth, even if the Koran had to be bent. In Europe the church proclaimed truth which must never be questioned.

The Baghdad brain trust wanted to know: Had God created the universe out of nothing, or had the universe existed from eternity in potentiality? Had God created it directly, or through intermediaries such as hierarchies of angels? Was each human soul part of a universal soul or was each soul created individually from nothing?

The Arab scholars translated and commented on the logic and opinions of Aristotle, Plato, Pythagoras, Euclid, and Hippocrates, as well as the sacred books of the Christians, the Jews, and the writings of other peoples. These Arab works would later form much of the basis of European scholasticism. Roger Bacon would say, *"Philosophia ab Arabico deducta est."*

In the process of studying philosophy, the Arab scholars branched out into mathematics, astronomy, physics, chemistry, medicine, and many other fields of knowledge.

There were not Arab astronomers, mathematicians, chemists, etc. There were Arab scholars with interest and understandings of many sciences. Europeans would speak centuries later of Leonardo da Vinci as the first "universal man." Not so. There were many universal men before him in the Arab world.

Arabs were brilliant in mathematics. They had to be to settle estates. A father might die and leave, say, fifty-three acres of irregularly shaped land to seven sons. Each was to receive exactly one-seventh of the legacy. The search for a better method of dividing inheritances led Arabs in the ninth century to advance the science of mathematics.

About A.D. 833, Khwarizmi, a professor in mathematics at the Baghdad school, collected and augmented concepts of algebra developed by previous Greek, Hindu, and Arab scholars. Khwarizmi and other Arab scholars used positive and negative signs and developed fractions much as they are used today. The Arabic word, *algebra*, which means *reduction* (solving of an equation) comes to us from the title of one of Khwarizmi's books. The study of algebra did not begin in Europe until the sixteenth century.

The Arab mathematicians at Baghdad also took the Hindu numerals, attached the zero (*cipher*—another Arab word), and produced the decimal system. Central American Mayans and Babylonians are also believed to have used the zero, but it was Arabs who gave the zero and decimal system to Europeans. European merchants quickly dropped the cumbersome Roman numerals and adapted "Arabic" numerals. No wonder. The number 1848 can be written in four figures in Arabic; in Roman numerals eleven letters are needed: MDCCCXLVIII.

Arabs also translated, interpreted, and advanced Hindu, Greek, and Roman findings in geometry. The Arabs showed how geometric symbols could be applied in many practical areas of life. They saw geometry, trigonometry and other mathematical sciences as essentially dynamic and expanding. Their mathematical work reveals the elemental relationship which Arabs saw between science and the Islamic doctrine of a dynamic, changing universe.

In sum, Arab mathematicians, by translating, interpreting, and adding to the ideas of Hindus, Greeks and other ancients, gave future astronomers, physicists, chemists, and other scientists tools with which to work. Arab contributions, translated from Arabic to Latin by European scholars (most of whom were churchmen) and with refinements and advancements by Europeans made the epochal works of Kepler and Newton infinitely easier. However, without the work of the Arabs, these two European geniuses, both of whom were devout Christians, might not have laid the foundations for space travel in the twentieth century.

Arabs were hardly interested in science for the sake of science. Some of their most remarkable discoveries and inventions resulted from efforts to meet practical needs of the Islamic religion. For example, the fast month of Ramadan was determined by lunar time, as was the entire Muslim calendar. The Muslim calendar is still today the only widely used purely lunar calendar, with its year varying from 354 to 355 days. The seasons and months bear no relationship, and there are around thirty-three Muslim years to every thirty-two Gregorian years.

When praying, a Muslim had to face Mecca. So astronomers fashioned instruments with which the direction of Mecca could be marked by a "mihrab," a semi-circle niche in one of the interior walls of a mosque, and to which Allah's subjects could turn wherever they might be at the times of prayer.

Caliph Mamoun built an observatory for the astronomers. Six hundred years before the Italian Galileo, the Arab Biruni proposed that the earth rotated around its own axis. At Cairo, the astronomer Yunus used the pendulum centuries before it was associated with Galileo. Yunus also compiled a set of astronomical tables far advanced from any previous calculations. At Toledo, in Spain, the Arab Al-Zarkali composed the famous "Tables of Toledo" which were used for centuries to determine planetary positions. He also devised an advanced astrolabe, an instrument used to measure the distance of heavenly bodies from the earth and for determining their positions.

Not until the sixteenth century did the Pole Copernicus utilize Arab translations and achievements in astronomy to help show that the sun is the center of our solar system. He is called today the father of modern astronomical science. His Arab predecessors, who translated Greek works on astronomy and made further discoveries themselves, are little noted.

Having seen Mecca, many intrepid Arabs wanted to travel further, and did. They produced road books unsurpassed for over two hundred years. They also wrote down observations of plant and animal life. This was how the Arab Baitar became the greatest botanist of medieval times.

The Arab Idrisi prepared for King Roger II of Normandy a magnificent world atlas with seventy maps, some of areas never before charted. This epochal work by an Arab is known today as "Roger's Book." Yaqut, the freed slave of a Baghdad merchant, compiled a geographical dictionary that also included extensive information on every field of science then known and the biographies of learned men. Arranged alphabetically, it was the forerunner of modern encyclopedias.

Because they studied the works of earlier geographers, the Arabs held some theories later disproved. For example, they believed the earth was divided into seven climates. But they thought the earth was circular, not flat as many Europeans continued to believe for centuries. Some Arabs located the summit or center of the world in India. Others said the center was at Mecca. This "cupola" doctrine was taken up much later by such Western scholars as Roger Bacon and Albertus Magnus. It was included in Cardinal Peter's book *Imago Mundi* which influenced Christopher Columbus to think that the world was pear-shaped and that there had to be a second world center in India at the base of the pear. The Spanish voyager was hoping to find India when he set sail across the Atlantic in 1492.

Arabs made many contributions to navigation. The magnet had been discovered by the Greeks and its directive magic by the Chinese. But Arabs were the first to use the magnetic needle in navigation.

Arabs were renowned as seafarers. In 1498 the Portuguese Vasco da Gama was the first European to find the way to India. He had an Arab pilot, Ahmad ibn Majid, to show him the way. The pilot followed an Arab map and navigated with the aid of maritime instruments used by Arabs five centuries before, of which Europeans were still ignorant. *Nadir*, *zenith*, and *admiral* are all Arab words.

Arabs took long strides in physics and the physical sciences. Al-Haytham of Cairo founded the science of modern optics when he proved that Euclid and Ptolemy had been wrong in claiming that light was emitted from the interior of the eye to outside objects. Al-Haytham showed it was the object that sent rays to the eye, in which its image was produced. From his studies on the refraction of light, Al-Haytham understood the principle of inertia on which Isaac Newton later formulated his First Law of Motion. Al-Haytham's *Kitab al-Manazir* (in Latin *Opticae Thesaurus*) became the basis of Roger Bacon's work on optics as well as later writings by Leonardo da Vinci and Johannes Kepler. In his monumental book, Al-Haytham described the eye's structure, optical illusions, binocular visions, comets, mirages and *camera obscura* (the prototype of the modern camera) which he invented himself. He also made an amazingly good estimate of the height of the earth's atmosphere and explained twilight by the refraction of light. Yet this Arab genius is not even mentioned in articles on optics in some modern Western encyclopedias.

Arab interest in physics centered on the interplay of forces that related to daily living. Fascinated by time, the Arabs devised clocks that moved by water, mercury and even by candle power. The great water clock at Damascus was regarded as one of the wonders of the world.

Arabs introduced the water wheel to Europe, which their ancestors probably invented. The three sons of Shakir described a hundred different water systems in their remarkable *Book of Artifices* (A.D. 860). The engineering trio designed water wells with fixed levels and showed how water could be raised by gravity. They created plumbing for hot and cold water and designed urban sewage disposal systems. By the eleventh century almost every major Muslim city had its own underground disposal system. In European cities wastes ran through open ditches.

The word alchemy (precursor of chemistry) is Arabic in

origin, as are the words alcohol and alkali. The most famous Muslim chemist was Hayyan, who lived in the eighth century. He may have discovered nitric and sulphuric acids. Arab chemists also rediscovered, or invented, alum, borax, and silver nitrate. They were familiar with many other chemical combinations which later passed on to Europe. Arabs also told Europeans how to extract sugar from sugar cane and how to make syrup (sherbet). Sugar and syrup are two more Arab words.

Arabs learned the art of paper-making from China. They had a large paper mill at Baghdad before the year 800. Europeans had never heard of paper-making then. Ceramics, crystals, fine pottery, embossed leather, damask, and countless ways of using precious metals for inlays were also introduced to Europe by Arabs.

Arabs were far ahead of most Europeans in agriculture. They knew pruning, controlled irrigation, fertilization, and other horticultural skills. One Arab agriculturist classified 585 plants. Arabs introduced to Europe through Spain spinach, asparagus, pomegranates, coffee, peaches, almonds, dates, oranges, apricots, and melons.

The Koran forbade the drawing of human or animal figures—a commandment some wealthy Arabs ignored by having hunting scenes and paintings of beautiful women on walls inside their homes. Public buildings and courtyards were decorated with carved lettering and unique classical designs of Arab script called arabesque. Arabic was the sacred tongue in which Allah had spoken to Muhammed. Arabesque was praise to the One God.

The pointed arch and vaulted ceiling, which later marked the Gothic style in Europe, was prominent in the Arab world. Arabs also gave European architects many more arches seen today in English, French, and Italian churches. Numerous other Arab architectural innovations are preserved in the older sections of European cities today.

Arab influence on Spanish music and dancing was greater than Spaniards will admit today. *Lute, guitar,* and *tambourine* are all Arabic words. Flamenco dancing was initiated in Spain when Arabs ruled that country.

The Arab Khaldun was the greatest historian of his time. Arnold Toynbee calls Khaldun's philosophy of history "the greatest work of its kind that has ever yet been created by any mind in any time." Before Khaldun, secular historians were mainly one-dimensional. They were occupied with the listing of rulers, empires, and dates and giving straight narratives of main events. Khaldun was the first to show that events did not happen in a vacuum, but were shaped by climate, social customs, religious beliefs, and many other factors.

The full sweep of Arab literature is yet to be revealed to the world. Arabic, as a language, is deeply impregnated with the spirit of the Koran and the religious life and history of Muslims. Translators say its many nuances and moods make it one of the world's most difficult languages to reproduce in other tongues.

Still, Arab literature has left many indelible marks on the West.

The most famous writer of the Arab period was Omar Khayyam, a Persian. Khayyam's *Rubaiyat* was translated from the Arabic by Edward Fitzgerald. A product of Arab culture, Khayyam was actually more famous as a mathematician. He prepared a calendar that may have been more accurate than the Gregorian calendar in use today.

The best known examples of Arab story-telling are in *The Arabian Nights*. Most of the stories in this anthology center around Baghdad and Cairo, although some were undoubtedly adapted from tales of India and other countries. Some literary analysts find themes from *The Arabian Nights* in Jonathan Swift's *Gulliver's Travels*, Samuel Johnson's *Rasselas* (a moral romance), Voltaire's famous satires, and many other works.

The Arab Yaqzan's *Alive Son of Awake* is often called the first real novel. Some literary historians think it was the prototype of *Robinson Crusoe*, while others tie the story to Alexander Selkirk who was marooned in a similar manner. The Arab story is about a baby shipwrecked on an island who grows up and develops a deep relationship with God. Before writing his classic, Daniel Defoe supposedly spent time in Morocco where he is presumed to have read the twelfth-century Arab novel.

The Italian Dante, as the outstanding figure of Italian literature, is judged by many to be the literary father of the European Renaissance. Dante drew from Muhammed's nocturnal trip to Jerusalem and ascent to Heaven, as well as from Catholic tradition for his *Divine Comedy*.

We have only hit the high points of Arab genius during the Golden Age of Islam. Horse breeding and horsemanship, artificial insemination of cattle and horses, the rites of knighthood, bullfighting, and much more came to the West from the Arabs.

Because there was so little travel between East and West and because Catholic authorities in Europe generally frowned on secular learning during the Dark Ages, Europeans did not know what the Arabs had accomplished until Catholic Crusaders began returning from the Muslim world in the tenth century with unbelievable stories. Then, Catholic armies captured the great cities of Muslim Spain in the twelfth century. Europeans who could read Arabic were overwhelmed by the treasures left by Arabs in libraries.

The far-seeing Archbishop Raymond immediately established an academy of translators at Toledo, much as Caliph Mamoun had done in Baghdad. Catholic scholars translated Arab works into Latin, the literary and religious language of Europe, with translations in national languages following. In this manner the legacy of the Greeks, which feudal Europe had neglected, and the scientific creativity of the Arabs came to the founders of the European Renaissance.

The Renaissance was in part a reaction to the rigidity of Catholic dogma and the papal bureaucracy. Such reaction and the rediscovery of learning caused many educated Europeans to reject the dogmas of Catholicism and become humanists. Their posterity strongly influences the world today.

But the Renaissance also stirred fresh study of the Bible in the original Greek, Hebrew, and Aramaic and the history of the first- and second-century church.

Translation of the Bible began in the languages of the European peoples. The invention of movable type made possible the spread of these translations throughout Europe. The result was the Protestant Reformation.

The Renaissance paved the way for the Reformation and provided the intellectual base for the great American experiment in democracy. The Reformation provided the moral and spiritual base for the Protestant colonizers of the New World.

These connections are well covered in American education and literature. However, the role of the Arabs in building Western civilization has been for the most part ignored and overlooked. The 1976 edition of the *World Book Encyclopedia*, for example, has a long article on the Renaissance in which the Arab role is never mentioned.

Similar omissions can be noted in some other reference works. The result is that most Westerners are appallingly ignorant of Arab accomplishment.

If we find it difficult to understand why this has happened, it is because we do not recognize the forces which influenced the writing of medieval and later European history. Thomas Carlyle's overstatement that history is "a distillation of rumor" is not far off the mark. Secular history in nondemocratic countries, ancient and modern, has always been written to the fancies of ruling powers. The glories of the ruler's country are extolled; failures and defeats are little noted or not mentioned at all. This is why the name of Moses is missing from the hieroglyphics of ancient Egypt.

European history in the Middle Ages was written to serve the policies of popes and kings. Islam was the enemy and could not be praised or credited for what the scholars of the Arab world had given Europe. Most historians only conveyed stereotypes of Islam and Arabs brought back by Crusaders while ignoring reports of Arab greatness.

Western ignorance of the Arab heritage has left a seedbed for the growth of prejudice and hatred against Arabs. A sad instance of this virulent anti-Semitism (remember, Arabs are Semites also) occurred in the eastern United States in 1978. Saudi Arabian Ambassador and Mrs. Ali Alireza offered to pay the asking price for the American Pharmaceutical Association building on Constitution Avenue in Washington. They wanted it for an official residence. They were told that the association's board would have to be informed first to see if the building could be sold to such controversial people. When the board okayed the sale, the Saudis were told that the association's membership had to be polled. When only 55 per cent of the pharmacists agreed, the executives said this wasn't a big enough majority.

Ambassador and Mrs. Alireza bought another house for a million dollars. But their prominent next door neighbor has gone to court to keep them from renovating the building. "It's not as though they are going to hang the laundry on the front lawn," gripes the Saudis' lawyer.

In New York, Prince Saud, the Saudi foreign minister, has had no better luck. The Harvard-educated prince's request to buy an apartment in one of the city's most prestigious condominium complexes was turned down.

Arabs have it hard in American education, too. Omar Rifai, a recent Jordanian graduate at Harvard, was quoted in *Time*'s education column as having to listen to some of his professors say "that the Arabs are cowardly, that we live in tents."

A visiting Palestinian professor at Harvard, Mahmud A Ghul, complained that Western educators still treat "the whole of Islamic civilization as a pale shadow of Western Christian thought. This is the academic version of the missionary or colonialist approach."

Thousands of Arabs study at American colleges and universities. Yet there are no tenured Arab professors in the University of Chicago's Middle Eastern study program and only one among a faculty of fifteen at the University of California in Berkeley.

Such ignorance and discrimination must not continue if the West is to have much influence in the Arab world. The patience of Arab intellectuals with the West is not inexhaustible.

7

Why Do Arabs
Mistrust Christians?

Westerners should seek more information about the Arabs and their accomplishments. But this will be only a start in understanding the grievances which Arabs—particularly Arab Muslims—have against Western governments and church bodies.

Why are Arab Muslims so mistrustful and fearful of Christian missionary work in the Middle East? Why are Arab nationalists, both Muslims and Christians, suspicious of peace initiatives from Western "Christian" nations?

We must grasp the answers to these questions if we are ever to understand the true basis for Arab resentment of the state of Israel. If we do, we will see that the Arab "grudge" is more against the "Christian" West than against Jews.

Furthermore, the questions must be considered

together. "To a Muslim, his government and his religion are inseparable," says Professor James L. Kelso, who has led many archaeological expeditions to the Holy Land. "He naturally assumes that . . . [our governments] and the Christian Church are likewise inseparable."

We will also better understand why Muslims believe that Islam is superior to Judaism and Christianity, and why Muslim families and communities so strongly resist the apostasy of individuals to these "inferior" faiths.

Consider:

There is not a single, visible organized church of Muslim converts in all the Arab world today, nor has there ever been in thirteen centuries. In some staunchly Muslim Arab countries, there is not today one Christian who will publicly admit conversion from Islam. There are known to be Christian believers in small informal house fellowships in strict Muslim countries, but they have not affiliated with any structured, recognizable church. Their social and political identity remains Muslim.

Arab countries with large Christian minorities connected to the historic churches are not nearly as "open" to the gospel as nations in Latin America and black Africa. One's religion is listed on his birth certificate and passport. This along with his name is a stamp of identity. There are also laws which make it extremely difficult to change one's religion, particularly if the switch is from Islam to Judaism or Christianity. And within the old Christian communities, there are strong pressures against individuals joining another church.

Take Jordan, one of the friendliest and most pro-Western Arab countries in the Middle East. The Southern Baptist Convention is the largest Protestant mission with twenty-nine representatives there. The missionaries are highly regarded. Yet President Carter's denomination reported in 1977 only seven Jordanian churches, 293 members, and $17,280 in gifts. Most of the members reported have family roots not in Islam but in the ancient Christian churches of the area.

Representatives of Western Christian denominations are careful to observe legalities. They are cautious about reporting Muslim converts. They speak only to trusted individuals and often end a story by saying, "Don't mention my name or even the country where the incident occurred. I could get sent home and the Arab believer might be jailed or even killed."

The following incident exemplifies the problems involved. Names and places have been changed for obvious reasons.

Abdul comes from a large clan that has been loyal to Islam for centuries. Like many other young Arabs, he moved from his village to work for a construction company in a large city. One day he answered a newspaper ad to enroll in a free correspondence course offered from another Arab country. The first lesson arrived by return mail. He completed it within a week and felt proud of his achievement. The second lesson came, then the third, along with a New Testament. He now realized it was a religious group sending the course; but there was nothing offensive, so he continued. Several months later Abdul checked "yes" to the statement: "I now ask Jesus Christ to come into my life and forgive my sins. I will become His disciple and follow Him as my Lord."

Abdul continued the lessons and wrote regular letters indicating more progress. After about two years his letters suddenly stopped. His correspondents wrote the employer Abdul had mentioned in a previous letter. "Abdul is our friend and once wrote us regularly. We're wondering if he might not have had an accident."

The employer responded promptly. "I'm very sorry to have to tell you that Abdul has become an infidel. Not only did he become a Christian, but even worse, he went around smiling and telling everybody about what he had done. I had to report him. The reason you haven't heard from him is he's in jail."

The missionaries heard no more for another two months. Then early one morning Abdul showed up on their doorstep. "I'm sorry that I must meet you like this," he said apologetically. "They let me out of jail on the provision that I would leave the country. I didn't know where else to go."

The missionaries took him in and helped him get employment in another Arab country. He is there today. His family has likely destroyed his birth certificate and disclaimed him forever.

By population ratio, far fewer Western missionaries, Protestant and Catholic, have gone to the lands of the Bible than to any other area of the world. And only a small percentage of these have worked directly with Arab Muslims.

The first missionary to Muslims was Ramón Lull. He was a wealthy poet and musician from the court of the king of Aragon when converted. Selling all his property and giving the money to the poor, he established missionary colleges for the study of Oriental languages, then went himself to North Africa around the year 1300.

Lull probably knew the Koran better than any other non-Muslim of his time. He challenged Muslim intellectuals to public debates. His popularity was so great that fanatics forced police to have him thrown into a dungeon, then banished. He was finally stoned to death by a mob in 1315.

Not for five centuries did another Western missionary venture into the Arab world. Henry Martyn was as brilliant and devoted as Lull. His cry, "Let me burn out for God," was repeated from thousands of Christian pulpits. He literally did, dying from heat prostration shortly after translating the New Testament for Muslim readers in Persian.

The missionaries who followed Martyn were militant and courted confrontations with Muslims. Keith Falconer, one of the most notable, declared: "There are weak points in Islam which, if persistently attacked, must lead to its eventual overthrow, while Christianity has forces which make it more than a match for Mohammedanism or any other religion. From its birth Islam has been steeped in blood and lust. . . . The Koran is doomed."

Such preachments in market places usually brought shouts and curses, volleys of stones, and a chase to the town limits. The missionaries took home hair-raising stories of danger and adventure.

Most Arab countries today will not allow direct proselytizing of Muslims. Many will not grant "missionary" visas at all. The undaunted come in under work permits, take secular jobs, and share their faith in free time. When this is not possible, some Western Christians may enter an Arab country as a tourist or student and distribute literature illegally. Several have been jailed for this or hustled out of the country for their own safety.

Why have Muslims been so consistently resistant to Christian missions?

Part of the explanation lies in Muslim pride and conviction. Says Dr. Warren Webster, a veteran of many dialogues with scholarly Muslims: "The Muslim feels that his is the last and best religion, the fulfillment of both Judaism and Christianity. Asking him to become a Christian is like asking a college graduate to return to kindergarten, when he has the latest revelation."

The Muslim's revelation is tied to clan and community. Islam is both individual and collective, personal and interpersonal. Dr. John D.C. Anderson, an English authority on Islam, suggested at an evangelical conference on "The World of Islam Today," that "one simple question" should be asked the persecutors of a Muslim who has become a Christian: " 'What is this man's sin, that you treat him so?' They might well answer like this: 'His sin is, first, that he is a blasphemer of our Holy God; second, that he is a traitor to our country and culture; thirdly, that by his apostasy he has brought great dishonor and disrepute on his parents, who not only brought him into this world, and taught him the true Islamic faith from his childhood, but who have given him love and care all his life.' And they would be sincere—and perhaps also right, according to their understanding. For the Christian has somehow produced the image of being not a true worshiper of Allah, but a blasphemer; not a good citizen of his country, but a quisling; not a man who honors his father and mother, but a reprobate son. . . ."

But this is not the whole explanation for Muslim opposition to Christian missions. We must also look to the tragic experiences of Arab Muslims with religio-politico Christianity in centuries past. Thus Ralph Fried, an early twentieth-century Christian and Missionary Alliance missionary in Palestine, wrote: "When we read of the persecutions of the Christians by the Muslim majorities, it would be a mistake to consider them equal to the persecutions of the early Christians who faced suffering and death for their personal love and devotion to Christ."

One of the most discerning Christian missionaries ever to serve in the Holy Land, Fried noted that "Christianity, after Constantine, deteriorated to a national, racial and religious-political movement in the East. . . . The persecutions and the resistance to [Christians] were more in the nature of a racial and national struggle for existence, though the underlying causes were religious."

Conflicts between certain Arab Muslims and Christian minorities, along with struggles between eastern and western divisions of Christendom, led to the Crusades. These ill-fated attacks by peasants and knights from the West in the eleventh, twelfth, and thirteen centuries are still bitterly hated by Arabs.

The Crusaders wore crosses sewn on their outer clothing. Today the "Red Cross" is the "Red Crescent" in Arab countries. The cross is a despised symbol. No Christian group would dare call a church meeting a "crusade" in an Arab city. One of Billy Graham's associate evangelists held a series of evangelistic services in cosmopolitan Beirut and recorded only one "decision for Christ." His reputation for leading "crusades" had preceded him.

The Crusades began in a time when great empires were dividing and falling and new ones rising. In 1054 the Eastern (Greek) Orthodox church broke away from the papacy. The Byzantine church, as it was known, already had a different rite, a married priesthood, and an aversion to imagery. But the major issue for separation, from the Byzantine perspective, was political pressure from the Vatican.

Mongol armies were forming in China. The fierce Seljuk Turks, who had converted to Islam, were restless in Central Asia. The Muslim caliphs at Baghdad and Cairo were struggling with palace revolutionaries. Muslim

Sunnite and Shiite factions were battling over questions of orthodoxy and descent from Muhammed.

The Shiite government in Cairo had captured Palestine from the Baghdad Sunnite Muslim dynasty in the tenth century. Until 1010 they continued Baghdad's policy of toleration and kept the holy places open to Christians, Jews, and Muslims. Then in 1010, a new Shiite caliph, Hakam, destroyed the Church of the Holy Sepulcher and began killing Jews and Christians. In 1020 he proclaimed himself the incarnation of Allah. He was shortly assassinated.

Taking advantage of Arab divisions, the Seljuk Turks moved out of Central Asia and captured Asia Minor (present Turkey) from the faltering Byzantine Empire. They overran Syria and took Jerusalem in 1071. They gave the Christians and Jews, who had managed to survive the persecutions of Hakam, no reprieve. Jews were compelled to wear black garments around their necks. Christians were forced to carry ten-pound crosses.

The Byzantine emperor swallowed his pride and asked Pope Urban II for help in driving back the Turks. Urban saw a chance for bringing the Eastern church back into submission to Rome. He also thought a military expedition against the Muslim Turks might unite the squabbling kings and nobles who were such a headache to him in Europe.

In 1095 he announced a great church conference at Clermont, France. In a stirring sermon, he described the persecution of Christians in Jerusalem and called for a crusade to rescue the Holy Land from the infidel Turks. Shouts of "God wills it!" and "We will fight to the last man!" resounded back. Urban's best preachers galloped from city to city, raising volunteers to "take the cross" and join in the holy war.

Undisciplined ranks of Catholic peasants flocked behind the preachers, pillaging and plundering Jewish homes along the way, demanding that Jews be baptized or die. None of the peasantry ever reached Palestine. Those who didn't starve to death were slaughtered by the Turks.

A corps of trained knights, coming behind the peasants, drove all the way to Jerusalem in 1099. The Muslims fought back savagely in hand-to-hand combat. After six weeks of hard fighting, the Crusaders entered the holy city. They massacred every Muslim they could catch. They burned the small Jewish community in its synagogue. They slaughtered large numbers of Eastern Orthodox, Armenians, Copts, and other Christians. Then most of the knights left for home, carrying heavy bags of rich booty. The rest remained to found the "Latin Kingdom," a string of four states running along the Mediterranean from Turkey to Palestine.

Fifty years later the Turks took back part of the Latin Kingdom. The Second Crusade, launched to recoup the losses, was a disaster. But the Latin Christians, as Roman Catholics still are called in the Middle East, held Jerusalem for eighty-eight years. It was recaptured for Islam by Saladin, a devout Egyptian Muslim general.

Saladin's name is still magic in the Arab world today. In a time when leadership was degenerating, he restored Arab pride. He was both a brilliant military strategist and a paragon of honesty and unselfishness. Among his close friends were Christians and Jews. Maimonides, the famous Jewish philosopher, served as his counselor and personal physician.

Instead of taking revenge for the Catholic massacre of Muslims, Saladin announced a general amnesty and religious freedom for all residents of Jerusalem. He also released thousands of Crusaders whom he had taken prisoner when the city fell.

News that the Muslims were again in control of Jerusalem raised new cries in Europe. Richard the Lionhearted of England, King Philip II of France, and Frederick Barbarossa of Germany led the Third Crusade to the Holy Land. Frederick drowned on the way over. Philip pretended to be ill and returned home to plot against Richard who had remained to fight. Richard defeated Saladin in several battles but could not retake Jerusalem.

The Fourth Crusade was supposed to be another attack against Muslims. Instead, the Crusaders attacked fellow Christians in Constantinople and unseated the Byzantine emperor from his throne. They took home tons of precious metals and art objects.

The so-called Children's Crusade, in 1212, was the most tragic of all. It was condemned by most churchmen, from both clergy and laity. Led by a visionary French boy shepherd, Stephen of Cloyes, one contingent set out from Marseilles, France, via seven ships which were provided for them free of charge. The children hoped to succeed where their elders had failed. Two of the ships were wrecked at sea, with all aboard lost. Survivors on other ships were, according to later sources, sold into slavery by unscrupulous captains. A second group of German children got no further than Italy where many died from hunger and disease. The rest returned to Germany.

The Crusades continued into the thirteenth century. Jerusalem was wrested once more from Muslim hands, but only for a fifteen-year period. Occasional intrusions were made in the fourteenth and fifteenth century with diminishing results.

The Crusaders did bring the Maronites and two other

ancient church bodies back into the Catholic fold. But by so doing they only added to the bitterness in the Bible lands. Many Muslims in Lebanon and Syria have never forgiven these fellow Arabs for embracing and helping the enemy.

Catholic Crusaders were successful in recapturing Spain from the Muslims. Here, too, they left a legacy of persecution and bloodshed which Muslims in Arab countries have not forgotten.

The Arab and Berber Muslims lost in Spain because of disunity. The decisive battle came at Las Navas de Tolosa. When the Arabs were pushed out of their section of the city, the Berbers refused to go to their aid. When the Berbers attacked, the Arabs looked the other way.

The disunited Muslims fell back from city after city. Pursuing Crusaders burned and looted behind them, massacring old people and children, and capturing young Muslim women for the sporting desires of the royal houses of Europe.

All of Spain, except Granada, was back in Catholic hands by the end of the twelfth century (Granada fell in 1492). King Ferdinand did not hate Jews or Muslims. He promised freedom of religion and security. But he had to keep the Spanish Catholic hierarchy happy to stay in power. Reluctantly, Ferdinand signed an order calling for Jews to convert or be banished. Muslims were given a little more time to see the light.

Many Jews submitted to baptism, but over 200,000 fled to North Africa. There they were welcomed by Muslims and given freedom denied in Catholic Spain.

The crackdown began on Muslims in Spain. A wood carving later placed in the Granada Cathedral depicted forced conversions. Monks were shown ripping turbans off humiliated Muslim men and pouring baptismal water on their heads. Behind the men stood their frightened wives, hiding their faces in shame.

The ignominy had only begun. A religio-politico intelligence agency called the "Most Sacred Brotherhood" sowed suspicions that Jewish and Muslim converts were continuing to practice old, forbidden rites. The "Inquisition," as the agency was later called, was given power to seize the property of anyone accused. Citizens who turned in the names of suspects were promised a portion of the confiscated wealth. The remainder was divided between the agency and the royal house. Whether proved guilty or innocent, the accused could not get their property back. The blessing of God was thus given to extortion. Almost everybody, except hapless ex-Jews and Muslims, profited.

Conviction brought the death sentence. The condemned prisoner was tied to a wooden stake, around which was stacked dry wood and kindling. If he recanted before the fire was lighted, the metal collar around his neck was tightened with a screw driver until he strangled to death. Then his body was burned. If he remained stubborn, he was burned alive.

The Inquisition was not new to Europe. The idea had originated in 1233 when Pope Gregory IX commissioned certain Dominican clergy to investigate heresy in the secret religious practices of the Protestant Albigenses in South France. In this situation, the pope went further than local bishops were willing to go. In Spain, over two centuries later, it was the reverse. The Spanish hierarchy pressured the Spanish monarch to mount an inquisition. Sixtus IV, the pope then installed in Rome, gave only reluctant, grudging approval.

By this time the glory of Islam was fading in the Arab world. In 1258 Mongol hordes from Asia had burned

Baghdad and massacred up to 800,000 Muslims. Christians, taking shelter in their churches, had been spared, perhaps because the Mongol ruler's wife was a Christian. The incursions continued. What the Mongols did not take, the Turks did.

The Turks had been converted to Islam by Arab Muslims in the seventh-century expansion after Muhammed's death. They retained much of their old culture. "A Turk before a Muslim," was a common saying among Arabs. "Treacherous" was another word applied to the Turks for their strategems in gaining power.

By the sixteenth century the Turkish Ottoman Empire controlled an area from North Africa to Hungary. The name Ottoman came from the Othman dynasty of Muslim rulers, who were called "sultans" instead of caliphs.

Some Turkish sultans were worse than Roman popes which they despised. They openly kept whole stables of concubines in elaborate harems, while some popes indulged themselves more privately. And they sold religious and civil offices to the highest bidders, just as some popes frequently did.

The Turks ruled more like the ancient Romans. Cities and provinces were left alone so long as they paid tribute and kept the harems of Turkish officials filled. Christians and Jews were permitted to live peacefully in separate communities called millets and practice their rites. Extremist Muslim sects were not suppressed so long as they did not force their beliefs on others.

Conversion of a Muslim to Christianity or Judaism was punishable by death in the Ottoman Empire until 1856. Foreign pressure from Protestant and Catholic countries forced the sultan to proclaim an edict of toleration. Protestant evangelists moved in and won hundreds of Muslims, including the private secretary to the sultan.

Then as dramatically as it had come, the toleration ended in 1864 and many of the new converts were arrested and sent into exile.

The largest community of Christians in the Islamic world was then the Armenians. They had maintained their identity since the first century and numbered around three million in the nineteenth century. The Turks lived in constant fear of an Armenian uprising and confined them to ghettos. In 1895 the Turks believed a revolt was brewing and massacred up to 100,000 Armenians. There was a second massacre in 1909 and a third in 1916 when no less than 1.5 million Armenian civilians were murdered in one of the worst genocidal atrocities of history.

The Turkish Empire was crumbling in the nineteenth century. Imperialist Czarist Russia was pushing down from the north, gobbling up territory like a hungry bear. Other European powers allied with Turkey in the Crimean War (1854-6) to keep the Russians from extending their influence to the Mediterranean. The Turks won that war but lost to Russia in the War of 1877-8. Again, the European allies came to Turkey's aid and forced Russia to give up much of her gains. None of this came free. Turkey's European supporters took large colonialist bites in the Arab Middle East. France got Algeria in 1830 and Tunisia in 1881, and forced Turkey to put Maronite Christians in charge of Lebanon in 1860.

The Lebanon power play was provoked by a Druze massacre of Christians. The Druzes had never forgiven the Maronite Christians for joining up with the Crusaders. From their mountain hideouts, the Druzes had been making occasional guerrilla raids for centuries. In 1860 they swept down from their mountain hideouts and killed thousand of Maronites.

The Muslims in the area sympathized with the Druzes. Turkish officials were caught in the middle. The French had strong religious and commercial ties with the Maronites, who had become the bankers of the Arab world. (The Koran forbade charging interest, so Muslims had allowed Christians to take this role.) Fearing annihilation of the Maronites, the French now threatened to take over Lebanon unless the Turks put Christians in power. The Turks capitulated.

The Turks also had a problem keeping peace among the Christian groups in Palestine.

At the rebuilt Church of the Holy Sepulcher, chapels were set aside for Eastern (Greek) Orthodox, Latin (Roman) Catholics, Armenians, Jacobites, Copts, and Syriac Christians. Fifty Muslim soldiers stayed constantly on guard with loaded rifles and fixed bayonets to prevent the "Christians" from fighting one another. After one melee between Greek and Latin monks, twenty-two monks and twelve priests were sentenced to imprisonment. A visiting American Jewish rabbi sarcastically remarked, "Jesus must have left Jerusalem long ago." It was no better at the Church of the Nativity in Bethlehem. Near the time of the battle in the Church of the Holy Sepulcher, two men were killed in a fight at the traditional site of Jesus' birth.

The Arab world continued falling under European influence. Libya became an Italian possession in 1912, and Morocco a French protectorate in the same year.

The Arabs could do nothing as they sank deeper into a sea of humiliation. The rule by Turkish quislings had been degrading. Now they were having to kowtow to Christians from the nations that in their view had murdered their ancestors in the era of the Crusades. Was this the will of Allah? Some could not believe it was. They huddled in off-street cafés and whispered of a time when they could hold up their heads in pride and praise to the God of their fathers.

Prospects for Arab freedom looked brighter early in the twentieth century. In 1908 a coalition of "Young Turks" revolted and deposed the old Ottoman sultan. Turkey was further weakened by a war (1911-12) with Italy which resulted in the loss of Libya. In two successive Balkan wars (1912-13), the Turks lost most of their territory in eastern Europe, plus Macedonia. Then World War I broke out in 1914, and the Turks allied themselves with Germany and Austria-Hungary against Britain and France.

Turkish control in the Arab world was vulnerable. The spirit of Arab nationalism was stirring. Young Arabs who had been educated in American missionary schools looked longingly to the United States. They were inspired by the ideals of self-determination expressed by Woodrow Wilson.

They sent feelers to British diplomats. "What are your plans for the Middle East if you win the war?" they asked.

The British knew what the Arabs wanted to hear. Top diplomats met separately with the two most influential Arab leaders, Feisal al Hussein of Syria and Aziz Ibn Saud from the small kingdom of Nejd in the Arabian peninsula. Feisal was a direct descendant from Muhammed; Ibn Saud was the hereditary leader of the puritanical Wahabi Muslim sect of Arabia.

"We'll give you arms, military advisers, and funds to fight the Turks," the British pledged. "When the war is over, we'll recognize your independence." They promised Feisal rule over Iraq, Syria, Palestine, Jordan, and Lebanon. They told Ibn Saud that he would have most of the Arabian peninsula. The British put their pledges in writing and the Arabs affixed their signatures.

The British knew the French had designs on the Arab world. Unknown to the Arabs, they struck a conflicting deal with the French. Except for Arabia, the Arab countries would be divided into British and French "protectorates." France would have Lebanon, Syria, and northern Iraq. Britain would take southern Iraq and Jordan. The future of Palestine, because of the interest of so many religious groups, would be decided by all the victorious powers after the war. This is known as the Sykes-Picot agreement. Arab nationalists still foam at the mouth when they hear it mentioned.

The unsuspecting Feisal and Saud turned their armies of twenty-five thousand men over to the British. Led by T.E. Lawrence ("Lawrence of Arabia"), the Arabs kept sizable Turkish armies tied down for the rest of the war, allowing Britain's General Allenby to win strategic victories in Palestine and Egypt. Britain had promised Egypt independence, too.

In November 1917, Britain played another deceitful card in Middle East diplomacy and promised in the "Balfour Declaration" to "facilitate the achievement" of a "National Home" for Zionist Jews in Palestine. This was done to win the support of U.S. Jews in the war. The full story of this promise, which Arabs would see as further betrayal, is related in the next chapter.

The Arabs had gone naively and believingly along. Then the bag of deceit began unraveling. The Bolshevik Communists, who had overthrown the czarist regime, opened the foreign archives of Russia and discovered a copy of the Sykes-Picot agreement. Then the Arabs learned about Balfour. There was nothing they could do but kick themselves and rage at the deception of "Christian" nations.

The dividing up was done in 1920—still remembered as "The Year of Catastrophe" in the Arab world. The diplomatic niceties of "protectorates" and "mandates" didn't disguise the reality that Britain and France wanted to keep the Arab lands under their thumbs. Only the Arabian peninsula, which nobody felt was worth much at that time, was turned over to Arab rule under King Ibn Saud. This was done in 1927—after Saud had already annexed another ancient Arabian kingdom.

The British and French did concede a limited form of home rule. Feisal was installed as king of Syria and his brother, Abdullah, enthroned in Iraq. But Feisal gave the French trouble and the French deposed him. When Abdullah began raising an army to restore Feisal, the European overlords became alarmed.

T. E. Lawrence and young Winston Churchhill persuaded Abdullah to let Feisal have his throne in Iraq. In exchange for this courtesy, Abdullah was given Transjordan, a desert territory divided by the Jordan River. The West Bank area included ancient Judea and Samaria with the cities of Jericho, Ramallah, Bethlehem, Hebron, and the old eastern section of Jerusalem where the chief holy sites of Judaism, Islam, and Christianity were located.

The rest of old Palestine continued under a British mandate and became the area which the Zionist Jews focused on for a homeland.

The embittered Arabs could not match the military forces of the European colonialists which remained to keep order. The masses could only riot and keep the pressure on for independence. Egypt won the first victory. The British reluctantly granted independence in 1922, but reserved the right to keep troops for protection of the Suez Canal. Iraq was next in 1932. Then

Transjordan declared its freedom in November 1941, when the British army was tied up fighting the Axis powers.

It was no surprise that the Arabs didn't support the Western Allies with much enthusiasm in World War II. Iraq backed Hitler and Mussolini until British military power forced a change of government. Syria and Lebanon collaborated with the puppet government of occupied France until Allied armies moved in and took over in 1943. Palestinian rebels received German military aid for raids on Zionist settlements and British soldiers. There was much trouble in Egypt where the people wanted British troops out.

Two of a group of young Egyptian military officers agitating for an end to British domination were Gamal Nasser and Anwar Sadat. Neither was enamored with Hitler. They hoped only that war pressure would drive the British out. This didn't happen.

Sadat had the worst luck. He became friends with a couple of German spies in Cairo. All three were reportedly betrayed by a belly dancer. Sadat was court-martialed and imprisoned. He finally managed to escape and spent the remainder of the war driving a truck in the slums of Cairo.

During this war period Arab leaders in various countries were too busy fighting their own battles to pay attention to Zionist immigration into Palestine. It was every nation and kingdom for itself. Freedom from European domination was the goal.

Too late, they realized that a foreign state was about to be planted in their midst.

Zionists saw it as a homeland in which they could live free from anti-Semitic persecution. Many Protestant evangelicals saw it as the fulfillment of ancient biblical prophecies. The British saw it as the way to solve their "Jewish problem." Americans saw it as restitution for the crimes of Hitler.

To Arabs the proposed new state of Israel was one more invasion from the Christian West.

8

What Price, Israel?

An explosion in a peaceful Arab village or Jewish kibbutz. Flying shrapnel and stone. The pounding of frightened feet on harsh desert sand. The shrieks of the dying and wounded. An old man blown into the street, his head nothing more than smashed flesh and blood and bones. A stunned child grasping for a foot that isn't there. A "retaliatory raid" or "terrorist attack," depending on who publishes the newspaper. It happens again and again and is served up to jaded Western TV viewers in living color on the nightly news.

The hijackings and assassinations get more attention. The massacre of Jewish athletes at the Munich Olympics warrants television specials. The bold rescue of hijack hostages by Israeli soldiers at Entebbe fuels books and TV dramatizations.

The wars arouse grave international concern. Hints of

nuclear war and Armageddon shake the world.

Refugees? Who cares? We saw others in the movie *Exodus*, in Biafra, and Bangladesh. Nameless, faceless drab figures in boats or tents. Palestinians? Hostages of wild-eyed Arab kings and generals who would rather see Palestinians rot than resettled in other countries. Salted with terrorists who spend days and nights dreaming of dead Jews. No matter that they've been homeless for thirty years.

High oil prices and oil boycotts are something else. They deflate the dollar, double the price of gasoline, and raise the blood pressure of angry Americans who can't understand how the Arabs can take our technology and be so ungrateful.

Added together, the problems emanating from the Middle East are causing a lot of people to take a new look at what's been happening there. Some for the first time—to the consternation of the government in Jerusalem—are having second thoughts about Israel. Is it worth the money—1.4 billion dollars annually in American aid—the trouble from the Arabs, and the peril of a world war to keep such a little nation afloat? Even some visitors to the Holy Land are wondering. A few return talking like author Elisabeth Elliot, who said, "You go to Jerusalem pro-Israeli: You quickly learn that there is another side, and you decide to be pro-Arab."

Israel, O Israel. Are you sacred triumph or unjust travesty? Oasis of hope or quicksand of despair?

Have we taken too much for granted?

It is time we get the facts. We no longer can afford emotions and slick clichés as substitutes for thinking.

The inquiring reporter immediately finds himself in a minefield: divisions are deep, opinions tightly drawn, old sores unhealed, and feelings raw.

Yet if we are to reach any conclusions and solutions for peace, we must try to answer the hard questions: How did modern Israel come to be? Why are the Arabs so angry that they have fought four wars with Israel?

Investigators have gone in two directions. Evangelical Christians have found what they believe to be answers in the Bible. Some have decided that the Irael born in 1948 is in direct fulfillment of prophecy, and that her conquest of Jerusalem had to be. Other evangelicals say that in the eyes of God, modern Israel is no different from any other nation.

We will pursue this debate in the next chapter.

For now, let us take a candid look at the founding of modern Israel. What moved the founders to fight for a Jewish nation after a dispersion of almost two millenniums? And why Palestine when more hospitable land could have been had elsewhere?

Jewish historians assert that their ancestors never stopped thinking of the land of their ancient forefathers. "Next year, Jerusalem" was plaintively expressed in millions of prayers.

Jews had different dreams. The Orthodox took the Old Testament promises of a return as futuristic: "Behold, I will take the children of Israel from among the nations, whither they are gone, and will gather them on every side, and bring them into their own land: And I will make them one nation in the land upon the mountains of Israel" (Ezekiel 37:21, Jewish Scriptures). The small Hasidim sect looked for a supernatural messiah who could come and lead this restoration.

Some great Jewish theologians and philosophers, such as Martin Buber, saw a messianic kingdom without a personal messiah. They wanted to establish in Palestine a colony of peace and justice. They believed this new

Israel—not necessarily a political entity—could be an eternal light to the nations—"a crown of glory in the hand of the Lord" (Isaiah 62:3).

"Practical" Zionists simply wanted a Jewish nation where Jews could find freedom and retain their identity.

Other Jews rejected the idea of a Jewish nation as inappropriate. They believed the best hope was assimilation and participation in democratic societies, particularly the United States. But they could not deny their heritage or common religious consciousness. If their persecuted brethren in totalitarian countries wanted a refuge, they would help them.

The sordid record of Jewish persecution indicates that Jews have as strong a reason to distrust Christians as Arabs. It explains why Jews have such a phobia about Christian evangelism. And it illumines the Jewish passion for a homeland.

A brief review of Christianity's long crime against the Jews is all that is possible here. Persecution arose in the second century after primary blame for the crucifixion of Jesus was shifted from Pilate to the Jews. The Roman historian Tacitus had plainly written: "Christ . . . was put to death as a criminal *by* Pontius Pilate." Justin Martyr, a Christian teacher, changed this to say: "This very Son of God . . . was crucified *under* Pontius Pilate *by* your [Jewish] nation." Jews began to be called "God's murderers."

Official persecution began under the first Christian emperor, Constantine.

Many of the Church "fathers" kept Christian animosity burning. Augustine said Jews were condemned to be servants to Christians forever. Cyril of Alexandria led mob attacks on synagogues. He was subsequently sainted by the Catholic church.

The Jews' only reprieve in the "Christian" Roman Empire came under the Emperor Julian. He promised to help them rebuild Jerusalem. Julian reigned only two years. For his kindness to Jews and other "unchristian" actions, including trying to revive the old pagan religion, which Christianity had replaced, he was labeled "the Apostate."

We have already noted that Jews fared better as "People of the Book" in the Islamic empire than in Catholic Europe. Jews under Islam in the Arab world generally reached intellectual heights not achieved again until the nineteenth century.

In feudal Europe Jews were classified as "aliens with special favor." Royalty and nobles made them a buffer class of moneylenders and merchants—"fall guys" for the upper class when the lowly serfs became restive over economic policies.

When rulers wanted more revenue, they raised taxes, forcing Jews to up their prices and interest rates. "Blame it on the money-grubbing Jews," they told the serfs. If a ruler wanted a larger safety valve, he had only to remove protection from Jews. They were easy victims for rioting mobs.

Because Jews were believed to prey on the poor, Crusaders en route to the Holy Land could rob them in good conscience. Jews were also ripe for other scapegoating. When a child turned up missing, Jews might be charged with killing the child in Passover blood ceremonies. Jews were also accused of killing Christ anew by stealing "hosts" (wafers) from Catholic churches and making them bleed. And Jews were blamed for poisoning wells, which was commonly believed to be the cause of the bubonic plague. Thousands were burned at the stake by Catholic vigilantes. The violence finally got so out of hand that the governments of England, Spain, and France banished Jews from their domains.

Through wanderings, intermarriage, and proselytizing, Jewish racial distinctions became blurred. Jews in Russia and Eastern Europe probably mixed with the Khazars, an ancient Turkic people whose leaders converted to Judaism in the early ninth century. Khazar ancestry may be more dominant than Hebrew lineage among Jews from this area today.

Jews in Germany, Italy, Austria, and a few cities in Poland were herded into ghettos during the Middle Ages. Later in Russia they were restricted to the Pale of Settlement. They had to wear a yellow star-shaped badge and three-pointed hat, and could only go outside during the day for employment. If a Christian approached they had to step aside.

Jews fared little better during the Reformation. Luther called them a "damned, rejected race" and approved the burning of Jewish synagogues and homes. Not until the nineteenth century did Jews get full citizenship in most European countries, although Holland gave them civil rights in the late sixteenth century. Many settled in Amsterdam and made that city a center of world trade.

The first Jews arrived in America a year after the Pilgrims. Mass immigration to the "promised land" of democracy came after 1880. Over the next forty years two million arrived from the Pale of Settlement where starvation prevailed. In the 1930s thousands more came from Nazi Germany. Among them were some of the world's greatest scientists, including Albert Einstein. Many went on to win Nobel prizes.

Even in America, Jews suffered from slander, discrimination, and occasional violence. Conservative Protestants were blamed the most for holding prejudicial stereotypes of Jews. A study by the Jewish Anti-Defamation League revealed that this group believed more than other Americans, for example, that Jews "did things to get ahead that Christians generally will not do." But in the main Jews were treated no worse in America than the first Irish immigrants.

Because Jews had freedom and opportunity in America, modern Zionism was born and nourished in Europe. Zionism—named for the ancient Hebrew word for Jerusalem (Zion—meaning "citadel")— gave birth to Israel.

The four major ideologues of Zionism were secular Jews. Moses Hess, called "our Communist rabbi" by his Jewish friend Karl Marx, wrote *Rome and Jerusalem* (1862), which summoned Jews to return to Palestine. Leo Pinsker, a Russian army officer, preached that a homeland in Palestine was the Jews' only hope for survival. Peretz Smolenkin, another Russian, believed that a Jewish nation could point the world to universal justice. These three were all dreamers. The fourth, Theodor Herzl, a Vienna playwright, was a man of action.

There might never have been a modern Israel without Herzl. And Herzl might never have become an ardent Zionist had not a French Jewish officer, Captain Alfred Dreyfus, been framed in Paris for espionage. The officer was later exonerated, restored to his position in the army and given the Legion of Honor. But the dreadful "Dreyfus Affair" convinced Herzl that anti-Semitism was a hopeless Gentile disease and the "Jewish problem" could only be solved by a Jewish state.

Herzl promoted and programed the First Zionist Congress in Switzerland in 1897. Here he boldly predicted that Zion Societies would "create for the Jewish people a homeland in Palestine secured by public law." Herzl was ridiculed and called a windbag. But he had a flag and a plan: Settle Palestine with Jewish agriculturists and skilled tradesmen; build Jewish national consciousness throughout the world; persuade a European power to protect the new state until it could stand on its own.

Ignoring the skeptics Herzl went from capital to capital, sometimes disguised as a journalist, seeking audiences with high officials. The German kaiser and the pope told him no. He got in to see the Turkish sultan, who then controlled the Middle East. But he was afraid to mention the idea after being warned that he might be killed if he did so.

Only the British were interested. Some London officials mentioned a spot in the Sinai desert. A water shortage and the disapproval of Britain's Agent-General in Egypt scotched that. Uganda was then suggested as a "temporary" home. Herzl couldn't get his fellow Zionists to agree to this, so he went on promoting Palestine. His slogan was: "Let the people without a land return to a land without a people."

Refusing to quit, Herzl returned to Italy where he saw the young reformist King Victor Emmanuel III in 1904. The Italian monarch listened, then remarked, "But Palestine is still someone else's [the Palestinian Arabs'] home." Herzl died before the year was out.

At the time of Herzl's death the Zion Societies were having little success in settling Jewish immigrants in Palestine. Jews then numbered no more than 5 per cent of the population.

The tactic was to raise money among European Jews and buy land—often from absentee owners who had obtained titles by bribing Turkish administrators. Often the Arab tillers knew nothing until the foreigners arrived with their documents. The occupants would protest that the land had always been in their family. The Jews would call Turkish authorities who would order the Arabs off the land. The Arabs would move in with relatives and plot to get the land back.

The settlers created economic problems. Jewish workmen were paid twice as much as Arabs for the same work. Arab laborers thought this unfair. And Arab landowners objected for another reason: The Jews paid higher wages than they did.

The immigrants had more money to spend. This, plus the building boom, fed inflation. The higher prices lowered the already low standard of living for the poor.

The Jews couldn't understand why the Arabs grumbled. "What are they complaining about?" they said. "Look what we're doing with this land. They can only benefit from our achievements." The Jews also thought the Arabs lazy and unimaginative. They didn't consider that the Arabs had been kept down under four centuries of Turkish rule.

There were culture clashes, though not with the small minority of Jews who had always lived in the land. Except for religion and strict monogamy, their mores were similar to their Arab neighbors'. But the European Jews had a different life style. Their women were more independent. Arab men feared their wives might be subverted by the new ideas.

Disquieting reports filtered back to Zionists in Europe who dreamed of a Jewish ideal in Palestine. Asher Ginzberg, a wealthy Russian businessman, who wrote under the name of Achad Haam, had begged the settlers to treat the natives "in a friendly spirit of respect." After an investigation he reported to friends:

"Our brethren do the opposite. . . . They treat the Arabs with hostility and cruelty, deprive them of their rights, offend them without cause, and even boast of these deeds; and nobody among us opposes this despicable and dangerous inclination. . . . We think that the Arabs are all savages who live like animals and do not understand what is happening around. This is, however, a great error." He wrote this in 1891. Twenty years later, when clashes between settlers and Arab resistance groups were more frequent, he declared, "I can't put up with the idea that our brethren are morally capable of behaving in such a way to . . . another people. . . . If this [restoration to the land] be the 'Messiah,' I do not wish to see him coming."

By 1917 the Zionist homeland in Palestine was still far from a reality. There were only fifty-six thousand Jews in Palestine, less than 8 per cent of the population, owning only 2 per cent of the land. But with a war on and Britain needing all the help she could get, there was an opportunity to make a deal.

The deal resulted in the statement, dated November 2, 1917, from Britain's foreign minister, Lord Arthur Balfour. It said in part:

> His Majesty's Government view with favor the establishment of a National Home for the Jewish people, and will use their best endeavor to facilitate the achievement of this object, it being clearly understood that nothing shall be done which may prejudice the civil and religious rights of existing non-Jewish communities in Palestine, or the rights of and political status enjoyed by Jews in any other country.

A story was floated in the Hearst newspapers indicating the promise had been given in appreciation for

Dr. Chaim Weizmann's contribution of synthetic acetone to the Allied war effort. Dr. Weizmann was an ardent Zionist and his invention vital for the manufacture of explosives. According to the Hearst report, the foreign secretary offered Uganda again as a possible Jewish homeland. The rest of the conversation supposedly ran something like this:

Weizmann: "Thank you, but if I were to offer you Paris instead of London, would you take it?"

Balfour: "But we already have London."

Weizmann: "True, but we had Jerusalem when London was a marsh."

According to the report, Balfour then wrote a letter to Walter Lord Rothschild making the pledge that became the launching pad for the state of Israel.

The Hearst story is disputed. What cannot be questioned are recollections by Lloyd George, the British Prime Minister in 1917, and young Winston Churchill.

George: "The Zionist leaders gave us a definite promise that if the Allies committed themselves to giving facilities for the establishment of a national home for the Jews in Palestine, they would do their best to rally Jewish sentiment and support throughout the world to the Allied cause. They kept their word."

Churchill: Recalling the "darkest hour of the war," the future leader of Britain said the Balfour Declaration had been worked out "not from sentimental motives [but] as a practical measure taken in the interest of a common cause, at a moment when that cause could afford to neglect no factor of material or moral assistance."

The Zionists did indeed keep their part of the bargain. For example, David Ben-Gurion, a Polish exile, went to New York and raised a Jewish legion that joined General Allenby's forces advancing in Palestine.

The Zionists were not entirely happy with the Balfour paper. They asked the British foreign office to substitute "the establishment *of* Palestine as the national home" for "the establishment *in* Palestine of a national home." They also wanted Transjordan, Mt. Hermon, and southern Lebanon included in the homeland. The Jews, like the Arabs, did not then know about the secret Sykes-Picot agreement with the French for the division of the Middle East. The requests were rejected.

Astute Zionists foresaw difficulty with the Arabs. They talked with King Feisal, who was expected to be the leader of a unified Arab state after the war. Feisal was reassured by the qualifier in the Balfour Declaration that said "nothing shall be done which may prejudice the civil and religious rights of existing non-Jewish communities in Palestine." He joined Weizmann in signing a friendship compact which acknowledged that the Versailles Peace Conference after World War I would set boundaries "between the Arab State and Palestine" and which pledged both parties to work for the carrying out of the Balfour statement. Two months later Feisal wrote Felix Frankfurter, an American member of the Zionist delegation at Versailles and a future Supreme Court Justice: "We Arabs, especially the educated among us, look with the deepest sympathy on the Zionist movement. . . . We all wish the Jews a most hearty welcome home."

Feisal evidently foresaw a Palestinian state after the war with a government representative of all residents, Jews and Arabs.

However, Feisal's attitude changed when the new Bolshevik government in Russia disclosed the secret Sykes-Picot agreement which called for continued colonial rule in the Middle East. From this time Feisal and other Arab leaders saw every Jewish immigrant admitted into Palestine as a political infiltrator from double-dealing Britain—a potential enemy instead of a welcome cousin.

At the same time opposition against the Zionist aim surfaced in the United States where Jewish sentiments were running strongly against a Jewish nation. American Jews feared a sharp division in world Jewry and a setback in gains made in their own adopted country. On March 5, 1919, Congressman Julius Khan from San Francisco, *New York Times* founder and publisher Adolf Ochs, the former U.S. Ambassador to Turkey, Henry Morgenthau, and twenty-eight other leading American Jews published a full-page protest in the *Times* against a Jewish state in Palestine. They claimed to voice "the opinion of the majority" of American Jews and asserted that only 150,000 out of 3,500,000 were Zionists.

The push for a state of Israel, they said, "not only misinterprets the trend of the history of the Jews, who ceased to be a nation 2,000 years ago, but involves the limitation and possible annulment of the larger claims of Jews for full citizenship and human rights in all lands in which those rights are not yet secure." They pointed to a "kindly spirit of warning" from George Adam Smith, the "greatest authority in the world on . . . Palestine: 'It is not true that Palestine is the national home of the Jewish people, and not of other people. . . . To subject the Jews to the recurrence of such bitter sanguinary conflicts, which would be inevitable, would be a crime against the triumph of their whole past history and against the lofty and world embracing visions of their great prophets and leaders.' "

Finally they asked that Palestine "be constituted as a free and independent state, to be governed under a democratic form of government, recognizing no distinctions of creed or race or ethnic descent. . . . We do not wish to see Palestine . . . organized as a Jewish State," they said.

The *Times* protest ran while President Woodrow Wilson was home on a break from the Versailles Peace Conference. During his absence the British and French announced the division of the Middle East that so infuriated the Arabs. Wilson was deeply disappointed at the "attempt to insert . . . the old reckonings of selfishness and bargaining and national advantage which were the roots of this war."

Wilson had tried to hasten the war's end by his "Fourteen Points" peace program. He made it plain that the United States would not be a party to a dividing of spoils. The twelfth point had excited the Arabs. It called for limiting Turkish control to Turks, meaning that the Arabs should be given independence.

Wilson had been a hero to the Arabs. An idealist, a man of prayer, and a devout Presbyterian elder, he deplored secret treaties and diplomacy based on expediency instead of morality. He believed that the day of colonialism was over. He felt that the best secular hope for lasting peace was a world community of nations in which the rights of all would be respected.

The Congress of Arabs met in Damascus after Sykes-Picot and the Zionist interpretation of the Balfour agreement became known, and issued a declaration: "We reject the claims of the Zionists for the establishment of a Jewish commonwealth in . . . Palestine. . . . We look to President Wilson and the liberal American nation who are known for their sincere and generous sympathy with the aspiration of weak nations, for help in the fulfillment of our hopes. . . . We should not have risen against Turkish rule . . . had it not been that the Turks had denied us our right to a national existence."

Wilson invited the British and French to join an Allied Commission of Inquiry to "ascertain the wishes of the [Palestinian] people. His European partners declined. Wilson sent two members of the American Peace Delegation anyway. They reported "anti-Zionist feeling in Palestine . . . is intense and not lightly to be flouted. No British officer consulted . . . believed that the Zionist program could be carried out except by force of arms."

The Zionist response to Wilson's "meddling" was to step up immigration. The native Palestinian Arabs rioted again and again. Hundreds were killed. It was the only way they could show their opposition.

The British began backing away from the Zionists. Churchill, now colonial secretary for Britain, denied a published assertion that "Palestine is to become as Jewish as England." Britain, he insisted, had "no such aim in view." Nor had his Majesty's Government "at any time contemplated . . . the disappearance or the subordination of the Arabic population, language, or culture, in Palestine."

Zionist leaders in Palestine were divided between hawks and doves. The doves' spokesman was Dr. Judah L. Magnes, revered founder of Hebrew University in Jerusalem. "The Jews have more than a claim upon the world for justice," he said in 1924. "But . . . I am not ready to try to achieve justice to the Jew through injustice to the Arab. . . . I would regard it as an injustice to the Arabs to put them under Jewish rule without their consent. If I am not for a Jewish State, it is solely for the reason I have stated: I do not want war with the Arab world."

Nazi persecution strengthened the position of the hawks and spurred immigration. From 1931 to 1939 the number of Jews in Palestine rose from 174,616 to 445,457.

Most came from Germany. But there were still more than twice as many Arabs in Palestine.

The Arabs fought back harder, raiding Jewish settlements and sabotaging British military installations. Arab terror cells were now operating clandestinely, seeking vengeance against the newcomers for both real and imagined wrongs.

Since 1920 a secret Jewish "defense" army called the "Haganah" had been operating in Palestine. In 1937 a secret Jewish terrorist organization called the "Irgun" began waging offensive war against both the Arabs and the British. The British were now being hit from both sides.

Young Professor Albert Einstein, a pacifist, was distressed. "I should much rather see reasonable agreement with the Arabs on the basis of living together in peace than the creation of a Jewish state," he wrote in 1938. "I am afraid of the inner damage Judaism will sustain, especially from the development of a narrow nationalism within a Jewish State. We are no longer the Jews of the Maccabee period!" Einstein warned that a return to the nation "in the political sense" would mean turning away from the spiritual nature of Judaism.

Dr. Magnes, theologian Martin Buber, and other Jews of like mind were equally distressed. They broke with the main body of Zionists and called for a binational Jewish and Arab state in Palestine patterned after Switzerland as the only hope for reconciliation of Arabs and Jews.

At the same time the British were feeling the heat from Middle Eastern Arabs and from 90 million Muslims in India, Britain's largest colonial possession. In a 1939 "White Paper" the London Foreign Office ordered Zionist immigration reduced to fifteen thousand a year for five years, then stopped. Five years after that an Arab state was to be established in Palestine.

Once again a world war helped the Zionists' cause. They pledged allegiance to the Allies when many Arabs were tilting to the Axis to show their disgust at Britain and France for not granting them independence. In the Allied countries the Zionists looked like heroes and the Arabs traitors.

The Zionists mounted opposition to the British "White Paper." The British would not budge. It was clearer to them now than ever that a Jewish political state in the heart of the Arab world would lead to a foreign policy disaster.

The Zionists pressed harder in Palestine where a young Polish freedom fighter named Menachem Begin had taken command of the Irgun. Begin mounted a savage campaign of harassment against Arab residents and British administrators.

Then the world learned that the Nazis had exterminated six million Jews in their death camps. How could this have happened in a "Christian" nation?

Revulsion and guilt blanketed Europe and America. Suddenly everybody wanted to help the Jews, especially the 200,000 or so survivors on evacuation ships.

Zionist promoters headed the ships into Palestinian waters. The British turned them back to detention camps in Cyprus—making Britain look like a monster to the world. President Roosevelt saw the dilemma in which the Zionists had put his ally. He offered to take half of the refugees if Britain would take the rest. By the time his envoy had returned to convey British acceptance, Roosevelt had reneged under pressure from American Zionists.

American Jews opposed to a Jewish state saw what was happening. "Why, in God's name, should the fate of all those unhappy people be subordinated to the single cry of Statehood?" cried Arthur Sulzberger, now publisher of the *New York Times*. "I cannot rid myself of the feeling that the unfortunate Jews of Europe's D.P. camps are helpless hostages for whom statehood has been made the only ransom."

In 1944 Zionist lobbyists got statehood for Israel into the presidential election platforms of both American political parties. Yielding to election politics, Roosevelt now pressed the British to admit 100,000 Jewish refugees into Palestine. The British refused. In Cairo the Zionist Stern Gang killed Lord Moyne, Britain's top official in the Middle East.

In September, 1945, the White House let news leak that President Truman, Roosevelt's successor, was preparing to issue a public statement on the future of Palestine. Clement Attlee, then prime minister of Britain, immediately warned Truman that any statement "could not fail to do grievous harm to relations between our two countries." He also told Truman that not all the refugees wanted to go to Palestine because all of the immigration certifications made available to them had not been accepted. The Zionists, Attlee said, were "insisting upon the complete repudiation of the [1939] White Paper." Attlee also opposed a proposal by Truman that Jewish refugees be given special treatment. They should be treated, he said, like all other refugees.

Attlee begged Truman to understand Britain's problem. "In the case of Palestine we have the Arabs to consider as well as the Jews." He noted that "solemn pledges" had been made by Churchill, Roosevelt, and by "yourself" that "before we come to a final decision . . . there would be consultation with the Arabs." Breaking these pledges, he warned Truman, would "set aflame the whole Middle East."

Britain's ambassador to Washington, Lord Halifax, was at the same time telling U.S. Secretary of State James F. Byrnes that disagreements on Palestine were "embittering relations between [us] at a moment when we ought to be getting closer together in our common interests." He said the Zionists were "using every possible form of intimidation to stop Jews leaving Palestine in order to go back to Europe and to play their part in its reconstruction."

Britain's Foreign Minister Ernest Bevin wrote Byrnes on April 27, 1946, that the Zionists were "acquiring large supplies of arms, most of them with money furnished by American Jews," and that Zionists were selecting new immigrants on the basis of military skills.

Three months later Begin's Irgun blew up a wing of the King David Hotel in Jerusalem, headquarters for the British administration. The ninety-one fatalities included some of the ranking British civil servants of Palestine. The British offered a reward of ten thousand pounds for Begin's capture. But the Zionist terrorism continued, with two British sergeants hanged in Jerusalem, the bombing of the British embassy in Rome, and letter-bombs mailed to Zionist opponents in Palestine and Europe.

An Anglo-American committee of inquiry investigated. Dr. Magnes risked his life by appearing before the committee and asking again for a binational state patterned after Switzerland. "The Swiss are divided by language, religion, and culture," he said. "Yet all these divergencies have not been obstacles to political duty." Magnes warned that relations between Jews and Arabs were worsening. Had the Zionist program contributed to this? he was asked. "There is no doubt," he replied.

The committee recommended that Palestine be "neither a Jewish State nor an Arab State." They predicted that any attempt to establish either state in the immediate future "would result in such civil strife as might threaten the peace of the world." The British mandate should be continued, they said, "pending the execution of a trusteeship agreement under the United Nations. . . ."

The British approved in principle the report and invited Jews, Palestinians, and representatives from the Arab League to join a conference. The Jews and Palestinians did not show up. Nothing was accomplished.

The next Zionist Congress refused even to discuss the inquiry committee's recommendations and demanded that Palestine become a Jewish commonwealth. Arab leaders countered with a call for an Arab state in respect of the population majority.

At this point, February 18, 1947, Britain turned the issue over to the UN and announced an end to the mandate in eighteen months.

The action moved to New York and Washington. A UN Special Committee on Palestine recommended separate Arab and Jewish states, with Jerusalem in an international zone. The Zionists decided this was the best they could get and began lobbying for U.S. support. At that time the U.S. could influence a majority of UN votes.

Zionist lobbyists worked hard on President Truman. Wrote Truman later in his memoirs, "I do not think I ever had as much pressure and propaganda aimed at the White House as I had in this instance." Truman became irritated to the extent that he refused to see any more Zionist spokesmen.

The U.S. Defense and State Departments stiffly opposed partition. Senator Howard McGrath, the

Democratic National Chairman, warned Defense
Secretary James Forrestal that the Democrats could lose
two or three pivotal states with large Jewish votes in the
next year's national election. Forrestal replied that he
would rather lose the states "than run the risks which
. . . might develop in our handling of the Palestine
question." Forrestal later reflected, "I thought it was
about time that somebody would pay some consideration
to whether we might not lose the United States."

The U.S. was in the heat of another election campaign.
Both parties again had Jewish statehood in their planks.
The Republicans accused the Democratic administration
of crawfishing from previous promises made to Jews.
Truman was a pragmatic politician and listened more to
his political advisers than to his cabinet members. A poll
now showed 80 per cent of American Jews favoring
Zionism.

Nevertheless, Truman insisted that his decision to
support the partition plan in the UN was based on
humanitarianism. His next secretary of state, Dean
Acheson, wrote that Truman was motivated by a "deep
conviction" that the Zionist cause was just. Acheson also
felt that Truman was influenced by his former business
partner, Eddie Jacobson, a passionate Zionist.

Truman was a Southern Baptist and had to also be
aware that many leading ministers of his denomination
believed the reestablishment of Israel was foretold by
Bible prophecy. During this time he talked with Jacob
Gartenhaus, a Christian Jew and head of the Southern
Baptist Home Mission Board's mission to American Jews.

Recalls Gartenhaus: "Prior to our meeting I sent him
my book, *The Rebirth of a Nation* [Israel] . . . . Among
Mr. Truman's first words to me was his expression of
appreciation of my book, with which he was greatly

impressed. Then the President wanted to know whether I, as a Jewish Christian, believed in the rebuilding of the Jewish homeland. My reply was that both as a Jew and as also a Christian, I believe in the Bible, which from A to Z revolves around the Jewish people and their destined mission as a regenerative nation in their regenerated and God-given Promised Land. When the interview came to a close that day, President Truman expressed what appeared to me to be appreciation of my views, with which he largely seemed to agree."

The Republicans had continued to criticize the Democratic administration for waffling. Truman made his final decision and instructed the U.S. representative in the UN to vote for the partition of Palestine into separate Arab and Jewish states.

The Zionists were permitted to participate in the UN debate even though they represented no member state. They talked about the persecution of Jews and ancestral rights.

Andrei Gromyko, the delegate from the Soviet Union, spoke in their behalf. "It would be injust," he said, "if we failed to take into account this aspiration of the Jews to a state of their own and denied them the right to realize it. The withholding of that right cannot be justified, particularly when we consider all that happened to them in the Second World War."

The Arab states were supported by only three other Muslim countries and newly independent India. They argued that they shouldn't be made to pay for the sins of Hitler. They said the partition plan would give the Jewish state over 56 per cent of the land. Jews then owned less than 10 per cent of the land. They said the UN had no legal or moral right to partition Palestine anyway. Would the U.S. or any other country permit the UN to divide its territory and establish a sovereign state within its borders? And regarding Jewish "ancestral rights," would the U.S. turn part of its land back to a colony of foreign Indians?

The Arabs never had a chance. They had no recognized political constituency in the U.S., nor a support bloc among evangelical American Christians (see chapter 9), nor money to buy a public relations campaign. (The year before, Golda Meir had raised 47 million dollars for the Zionist cause!) They did not enjoy cultural rapport with Westerners as the Zionists who had been educated in the West did. Most damaging to their cause, they were opposed by the two great world powers, the U.S. and the Soviet Union.

When the outcome was obvious, Muhammed Khan, foreign minister of Muslim Pakistan, stood in the UN and warned his free world allies: "Remember that you may need friends tomorrow . . . in the Middle East. I beg of you not to ruin and blast your credit in these lands."

The motion for partition passed easily on November 29, 1947. Four days later the British announced they would pull out the following May 15, weeks ahead of schedule. The Arab countries declared that they would defend their rights.

The violence escalated. On March 19, 1948, the U.S. told the UN Security Council that the Partition Resolution could not be implemented by peaceful means. In the event of trouble, the U.S. delegate anticipated that the Russians would try to be part of a UN peacekeeping force, and the U.S. did not want Russians in Palestine. The U.S. delegate asked the Security Council to recommend to the General Assembly a temporary UN trusteeship for Palestine.

On March 24, the Jewish Agency for Palestine rejected

the trusteeship proposal. They would not consider any postponement of a Jewish state in Palestine. That evening racketeer Mickey Cohen hosted a private Hollywood party that raised $375,000 for "Hebrew freedom" in Palestine.

The following week a shipload of arms from Communist Czechoslovakia arrived for Zionist use in Palestine against the Arabs.

On April 10, 1948, the Irgun, still under Begin's command, the Haganah, and the so-called Stern Gang occupied the small Arab village of Deir Yassin. The village was inside the Jerusalem "International Zone" so designated in the UN Partition Resolution. After the Haganah left, the Irgun and the Stern Gang butchered 254 Arab men, women, and children and threw their mutilated bodies into a well. Then they called a press conference and pronounced the massacre a "victory" in the war to unify Palestine. Many Zionist hawks condemned the atrocities.

This massacre put thousands of Arab civilians to flight. Begin later wrote that as a consequence of Deir Yassin, the Arabs "were seized with limitless panic and started to flee for their lives . . . even before they clashed with Jewish forces."

The British mandate had a month to go and the Haganah was on the offensive. Jaffa, Acre, Haifa, the western part of Jerusalem, Safad, and Tiberias fell in rapid succession to trained Jewish fighters from over fifty countries. Tens of thousands of Arabs left their homes with little more than the clothes on their backs and fled into newly independent Jordan (formerly Transjordan).

Dr. Magnes flew to Washington and urgently sought an appointment with General George Marshall, the secretary of state. Marshall said afterwards, "It was the first talk on Palestine in which I had complete trust."

Marshall got Magnes into the Oval Office. The educator had given up hopes for a binational state. He was pleading now for a truce and some kind of settlement before the inevitable happened. Truman listened, but in an election year he was taking no chances. The entire conversation, he said, must be off the record.

The UN was alarmed and on May 14 appointed a mediator between the Jews and Arabs, Count Folke Bernadotte, the respected former president of the Swedish Red Cross. He left that same day.

Truman, on the advice of lawyer Clark Clifford and others, had already sent word to Dr. Weizmann and Ben-Gurion. They should go ahead on May 14 and declare statehood, he said. He would announce U.S. recognition as soon as the news reached Washington.

Armies from neighboring Arab states were poised at the borders of Palestine, awaiting only the end of the British mandate. Three hundred thousand Palestinian refugees were already in Jordan.

At 4:00 P.M. Jerusalem time (midnight in Washington) the Jewish National Council convened in the Tel Aviv Museum. It was too dangerous to meet in Jerusalem. The Jewish Philharmonic Orchestra played the chosen national anthem. Ben-Gurion, "the prophet with a gun," stepped in front of a large photograph of Herzl and read the declaration. Venerable Rabbi Maimon thanked "the God of Abraham, Isaac, and Jacob" for "sustaining us so that we have lived to see this day."

Ben-Gurion signed, then the other Council members affixed their signatures. "The State of Israel is now in existence," Ben-Gurion, the first prime minister, declared in a choked voice. "The meeting is now adjourned."

In the streets of Tel Aviv Jewish crowds sang and danced and cried for joy. Leaders of the new state proudly forecast a nation of ten million with boundaries far beyond the present borders.

At fifteen minutes past midnight, Washington time, President Truman announced diplomatic recognition. The Soviet Union soon followed.

By midnight in Palestine Arab and Jewish armies were locked in battle.

Count Bernadotte, the UN mediator, arrived and managed to arrange a temporary truce. Then he filed this report to the UN:

"The Jewish state was not born in peace . . . [but] in violence and bloodshed. . . . No settlement can be just and complete if recognition is not accorded to the rights of the Arab refugee to return to the home from which he has been dislodged by the . . . armed conflict between Arabs and Jews. . . . It would be an offence against the principles of elemental justice if these innocent victims of the conflict were denied the right to return to their homes while Jewish immigrants flow into Palestine. . . ."

Count Bernadotte's solution was: "The Arab areas of Palestine should be joined with Jordan, which should then form a Union with Israel. The Union should handle economic affairs, foreign policy, and defense for both Israel and Jordan while each remained free to control its own internal affairs."

Both Israel and the Arab countries rejected the proposal immediately. The fighting resumed. The Israelis captured more territory.

On September 17, the UN mediator and his assistant were killed in Jerusalem by men wearing Israeli army uniforms. Ben-Gurion ordered members of the Stern Gang arrested. The assassins were never caught. A few

146

months later a leader in the gang, Nathan Yeldin-Mor, won a seat in the Israeli Parliament.

Judah Magnes was still in New York. He was now pleading the plight of the Arab refugees. In his last article, published in the October 1948 issue of the Jewish opinion magazine *Commentary*, he lamented: "It is unfortunate that the very men who could point to the tragedy of Jewish displaced persons as the chief argument for mass immigration into Palestine, should now be ready, as far as the world knows, to help create an additional category of displaced persons in the Holy Land—the Palestine Arabs!"

One of Magnes' last pleas was to the Jewish Joint Distribution Committee for help to the refugees. He had helped create this agency which had aided thousands of displaced Jews. When his entreaty was ignored, he resigned, saying, "This could have been the most glorious chapter in the glorious history of the 'Joint.' " He died a few days later—some said of a broken heart.

On November 16, when it was clear that the Arab armies had lost, the UN called for an armistice. The fighting ebbed. It was now evident that the Arabs had been beaten badly. Despite their larger civilian populations, they had mustered only 55,700 soldiers for the fighting against 120,000 trained Israeli fighting men from fifty-two countries. Some of the Israelis had fought in Ben-Gurion's legion beside the British. Not only had the Arabs been outnumbered, they had been without a common flag or anthem against an enemy with a strong martial spirit.

On December 11 the UN adopted a resolution concerning the 700,000 Palestinians dispossessed of their homes: "Resolved that the refugees wishing to return to their homes and live at peace with their neighbors would be permitted to do so at the earliest practicable date, and that compensation should be paid for the property of those choosing not to return and for loss of or damage to property. . . ." This resolution would be reaffirmed year after year by the UN General Assembly but never implemented.

Israel now controlled 22 per cent more territory than the area allotted to the Jewish state in the UN partition plan. She refused to surrender this additional land.

But she was anxious to be admitted to the UN and agreed to meet with a UN Conciliation Commission at Lausanne, Switzerland. With Arab representatives present, a protocol was drawn for future peace negotiations. To the protocol was attached a map showing the boundaries specified in the UN plan before Israel had taken the additional land. Israel signed the protocol on May 12, 1949, the day after she had applied to the UN. As soon as her application was accepted, the Israeli government unilaterally revoked the Lausanne agreement.

Where hundreds of thousands of native Palestinians had once lived, there were now only vacant houses and farms. Begin implored world Jewry, "Quickly, quickly! Our nation has no time. Bring in hundreds of thousands of immigrants. We are now in the midst of a war for survival." Exactly 736,358 Jews arrived within six years of statehood. The largest proportion came from countries with a long history of Jewish persecution—Rumania, Poland, Hungary, and Russia. The fewest came from the U.S. and Canada.

Most of the new immigrants settled on "abandoned" Arab property. Of the 370 new Jewish settlements established between 1948 and early 1953, no less than 350 were on such property. By 1954 over one-third of Israel's

Jewish population had occupied property owned by displaced Arabs.

While the emigrant population was doubling, Jewish agencies in the U.S. and western Europe pushed bond selling and fund drives to finance development in Israel. Interest on the bonds was declared tax exempt in the U.S.—something never before granted to a religious group. Between 1948 and 1968 the United Jewish Appeal raised over 4 billion dollars in the U.S. for Israel while only 8,800 American Jews emigrated there. Most of these later returned to the U.S.

The refugees were quartered in UN camps. Except for the Arab states who had been decisively whipped in the 1948 war, few voices were raised in their behalf. The most plaintive plea came from the IHUD Association of Israel: "In the end we must come out publicly with the truth, that we have no moral right whatever to oppose the return of the Arab refugees to their land . . . that until we have begun to redeem our sin against the Arab refugee, we have no right to demand that American Jews leave their country to which they have become attached and settle in a land that has been stolen from others, while the owners of it are homeless and miserable. . . . In the end we must speak the truth. We are faced with this choice: To listen to the voice of truth for the sake of our own good and genuine peace, or, not to listen to it, and to bring evil and misfortune upon us and the future generations."

There would be other voices raised from thoughtful, worried observers. Historian Arnold Toynbee would later tell McGill University students in Montreal, "The treatment of the Palestinian Arabs . . . was as morally indefensible as the slaughter of six million Jews by the Nazis. . . ." The Palestinians, Toynbee said, had been "robbed" of their territory. Though not comparable in numbers to the crimes of the Nazis, it was comparable in quality, he declared. Typical Zionist response to such statements came from a rabbi who said, "The more one reviews his [Toynbee's] statements, the more one realizes that he is not a friend of the Jewish people, and that his desire is to do away with them."

The same month Toynbee spoke to the students (May 1961), he told the annual meeting of the American Council for Judaism in Philadelphia, "Zionism and anti-Semitism are expressions of an identical point of view. The assumption underlying both ideologies is that it is impossible for Jews and non-Jews to grow together into a single community, and that therefore a physical separation is the only practical way out. The watchword of anti-Semitism is 'Back to medieval apartheid'; the watchword of Zionism is 'Back to the medieval ghetto.' All the far-flung ghettos in the world are to be gathered into one patch of soil in Palestine to create a single consolidated ghetto there."

But in the glow of victory and the challenge of a land of their own, the Jewish militants of the new state were not thinking of the philosophical and historical implications of what they had accomplished. The farmers were making the desert bloom on land once tilled by Arabs. The engineers were building new cities. The generals were shoring up border defenses. The fund-raisers and lobbyists were soliciting more aid from America. All while the refugees languished and the newly independent Arab countries seethed in shame and frustration over what they saw as the new outpost of colonialism in their midst.

9

The Palestinians: Key to Peace?

Anis Shorrosh* is a Palestinian Arab, a native of Nazareth, the hometown of Jesus, a graduate of New Orleans Baptist Theological Seminary, and a Southern Baptist evangelist with impeccable credentials and unquestioned integrity.

He was a fifteen-year-old boy in 1948. His Shorrosh clan of the Christian Rehani tribe had lived in the Arab hometown of Jesus for hundreds of years. His family was Greek Orthodox until Baptist missionaries came to Palestine early in the twentieth century. His grandmother had been a well-known "Bible woman" and teacher of the Scriptures; his father, Agustine, the first Arab Baptist preacher in the area.

In 1948 the population of Nazareth was about evenly divided between Muslims and Christians of all denominations. The Shorroshes attended the small

---

* The dramatic story of Anis Shorrosh is more fully told by the authors in *The Liberated Palestinian*, published by Victor Books, a division of Scripture Press, Inc., Wheaton, Ill.

Baptist church near the traditional Mary's Well on the main road to Cana.

Anis remembers vividly the tense fear-filled weeks that preceded the fall of Nazareth. Refugees fleeing towns already occupied by Jewish soldiers passed daily. Many carried only the clothes on their backs. He saw one man in pajamas.

The Nazarenes kept expecting Syrians to come to their rescue. The only "Syrians" that came were Jewish soldiers in tanks disguised with Syrian markings. The people went out to welcome them and ran in panic when they realized the trick.

Agustine Shorrosh was returning from a trip to Acre. Anis's mother and three of her children hid in a cave. They heard gunfire and explosions all night and thought the town was being destroyed. When the battle finally died down they fled on camels across the Jordan River into Jordan where thousands of other refugees were going. They were among the fortunate few who had relatives in Jordan and did not have to move into one of the hastily set up UN tent camps.

Before leaving Nazareth, Anis knew that a cousin had been cut in two by Israeli guns. After reaching Jordan, he heard that his father had also been killed while trying to get back to his family.

In the immediate weeks following, the Shorrosh family clutched at every scrap of news brought by refugees still coming out of the Israeli-occupied areas. They were told that another cousin had been killed in Jerusalem, and that the Jews had claimed their house in Nazareth. At Christmas they heard over the radio of UN Resolution 194 which said the refugees should be allowed to return in peace and receive payment for damaged property, or be paid for their property if they chose not to go back. But as the months passed, the resolution was not implemented. There were no peace settlements, no agreement on boundaries, and no chance to return.

The "temporary" status of the 630,000 refugees in Jordan dragged on. The Shorroshes were living in one room. Anis did odd jobs in his Uncle Tamin's shop. But it was not enough and the family finally had to apply for a UN food ration card. UNITED NATIONS RELIEF AND WORK AGENCY was stamped on one side and their names on the other. It was their only proof of existence. They, with the thousands in the squalid tent cities, were a people without citizenship, passports, or homeland.

Month after dreary month passed. Anis had no father, no country, no home, no education, no regular employment, no future. Like other young Palestinian men, he hungered for revenge. He thought if he could just get a machine gun, he would slip across the border, kill as many Jews as he could, and go down fighting. But there was no gun and no opportunity for vengeance. In despair he ran into the desert, where Jacob had wrestled with an angel, and lay down amidst the rocks.

All night and into the next day he lay there. Hate so consumed him that he cried to die. By the next afternoon his vision was blurred and his tongue swollen. Half delirious, he remembered teachings from the Baptist Sunday school and thought, "This must be what hell is like."

He couldn't take a chance on hell. Somehow he managed to stumble home and into the arms of his mother. He spent the next day, Easter Sunday, reading his mother's Bible. "God, if you're real, please help me," he begged. "I'll give you my life."

Miraculously, it seemed, he was hired as a lab

technician at the Baptist mission hospital in Ajlun, Jordan. Here he so impressed the mission staff with his sharp intellect that they wrote Baptist educators in the U.S. recommending him for a scholarship. Clark College arranged for his flight to the U.S. and a grant to complete high school and college in Mississippi. While in college he felt a call to preach. He went on to seminary and then entered full-time religious work as an evangelist.

Anis is no political activist, but he takes every chance to enlighten Americans on the plight of the Palestinians, which he believes continues as the central problem of the Mideast tragedy. He says:

"The Israelis claim that Palestine is theirs because God gave the land to Abraham and his descendants. But Arabs also are descendants of Abraham and entitled to remain in the land they have occupied for centuries.

"The Jews talk about the vast improvements they had made in the land. Arabs say they could have done the same with aid from the U.S. and the UN.

"Israelis say the UN gave them the land, making them the legal owners. Arabs ask, 'Who gave Palestine to the UN? Let the UN give them some other land that is not occupied.'

"They were robbed of their land thirty years ago. They're still living in camps on handouts from the UN. Can you imagine how it feels to be exiled from home? To mourn for loved ones who were killed for no other reason than that they lived in a land which foreigners wanted? To stand in a ration line for hours to get a measure of flour? To have no work, no property, no hope?

"Every year the UN reaffirms the resolution to return. Nothing happens. Nothing. The Palestinians continue as pawns in a situation which they did not create. Why should they be punished for what Europeans did to the

Jews so long a time ago?

"Where is truth and justice? Is it right for one people to displace another, just because they have powerful friends who will give them arms and money and guarantee their security? Is it right?"

Anis Shorrosh does not endorse the extreme violence of Palestinian *fedayeen* ("fighters for a cause"). But after Senator Robert Kennedy was killed by Sirhan Sirhan, a Palestinian refugee, he wept before a Baptist congregation in Texas. "Here, but for the grace of God, stands another Sirhan Sirhan," he sobbed. "If I had not become a Christian believer, I might have done the same thing. Please listen to what this young man and other Palestinians are trying to tell the world. They are saying, 'Look at us! We are people driven from our lands. Don't pretend we don't exist. Help us.' "

A corps of articulate, well-educated, Arab-Americans are also trying to wake up the West. Two examples:

Dr. Ibrahim Abu-Lughod, professor of political science at Northwestern University in Evanston, Illinois, told the Committee on International Affairs of the U.S. House of Representatives, September 30, 1975: "The historical record of the Middle East suggests clearly that an American policy wedded to Zionist premises, over-sensitive to Israeli aspirations and needs, and betraying total neglect, national denigration, and hostility to the Palestinians is counterproductive to peace, stability, and good relations between the Arab and the American peoples. . . . Continuation of such a policy . . . is blind to the centrality of the Palestinians to the Arab-Israeli conflict and totally rejects their aspirations and internationally sanctioned rights. It will undoubtedly lead to further instability."

Dr. Hisham Sharabi, professor of history at

Georgetown University in Washington, D.C., and editor of the *Journal of Palestine Studies*, spoke to the Senate Subcommittee on the Near East the same day: ". . . It is not the number or firepower of the Palestinians which make them so crucial to peace and stability in the Middle East. In the Arab world the Palestine problem is not the Palestinians' problem merely, but an overall Arab problem. It is deeply embedded in the national psyche, and no political leader can take a position on it which does not have the consent of the Palestinians. No Arab state can by itself agree to a settlement to which the Palestinians do not subscribe."

Senator James Abourezk, U.S. Senator from South Dakota, born in South Dakota of Arab descent, said at the time of the 1974 oil boycott: "The dispossession of the Palestinian refugees remains the root of the Middle East problem. The cause of all the Arab-Israeli wars since 1948 is, in my opinion, ultimately traceable to the forcible eviction of the Palestinians from their homes and their subsequent existence in miserable refugee camps. From the refugee camps—with poor sanitation, inadequate food and shelter, and scarce jobs—have sprung anger and bitterness that will not be easily quieted."

The dispossessed Palestinians themselves give more concise opinions. One says: "Our problem is simple: The foreigner took our land and kicked us out. We want to return. We're not anti-Semitic, for we're Semites ourselves. We're not anti-American. But by continuing to support Israel, you're pushing us into the hands of the Russians." Another asks: "How would you feel if your little girl was forced to hold out her hand every day for half an orange when her grandfather in Palestine once owned orange groves?"

There are also responsible present-day Israeli leaders

who recognize that Palestinian rights must be restored before there is to be peace in the Middle East. They seek reconciliation through compromise and prefer diplomacy to military action. They believe there is a Palestinian people which has the right to self-determination. They contend that the first priority of Israeli foreign policy should be to deal with the Palestinians as a people and not as enemies. One of the most prominent is Amos Kenan, who once belonged to the notorious Stern Gang and is now a prominent playwright and novelist. Kenan participated in a panel discussion (published by Breira Inc. of New York City) with other Israelis on "Israel and the Palestinians." He said in part:

". . . The reality today is that there is a Palestinian people and there is an Israeli entity and the main problem of the dispute is no longer that of the self-identity of each side but of the right of both sides to self-determination, and the right of each side to live here while fully recognizing the rights of the other side to do likewise.

". . . We are talking here only of 2.5 million Palestinians, but for the 100 million Arabs, those two-and-a-half million Palestinians are a symbol and a challenge against an entire culture that oppressed the Third World. The entire struggle of the Arabs focuses on and is symbolized by the Palestinians."

Speaking in the same symposium, Mattityahu Peled, a former major-general in the Israeli army and now head of the Faculty of Arabic Studies at Tel Aviv University, agreed that the question of whether there is a Palestine people can no longer be argued. "Before . . . 1967 many of us truly believed the theory that there is no Palestinian people and that there was only the 'Palestinian trump card' which the Arab countries play for their own convenience. . . . In 1967 we learned suddenly that this 'trump card' is not merely empty but that what is behind it is a most most serious and concrete entity. . . . Instead however, the Israeli government, as we know, tried to ignore this fact which had suddenly been revealed, by promoting all kinds of baseless formulae in the wake of which we find ourselves in the present situation, when not only is it no longer possible to debate whether or not there is a Palestinian people, but it is absolutely clear and agreed by the whole world that this people exists and has rights, and that no settlement in the Middle East can be reached which fails to take into account the existence and rights of this people."

As well qualified as they are, such persons are seldom quoted in Western newspapers and interviewed on television. For most Westerners, the message and goal of the Palestinians is encapsuled in one man: Yasser Arafat, veteran guerrilla fighter and director of the Palestine Liberation Organization (PLO), which scores of nations recognize as the Palestine government-in-exile. Like him or not, Arafat is principally responsible for forcing the Arab governments, Israel, and the world to deal with the Palestinian question. A bachelor who does not drink or smoke, he is "married" to the cause. Should the Palestinians attain statehood, he will probably be honored as the father of their country.

It is essential that we understand Arafat and his rise to leadership of the Palestinian movement. He may not speak for all the Palestinians, or even the majority, but the world spotlight focuses on him more than any other.

PLO press releases have him born in Jerusalem about 1930. Arafat laments in sad pride that his home was one of the 129 Arab houses bulldozed at the end of the Six-Day War in 1967 to make a plaza before the Wailing Wall. Relatives, however, say he was born in Cairo. No matter.

His pedigree on both sides is Palestinian, Arab, and Muslim, and he grew up on the volatile Gaza Strip. His father was a merchant in Gaza with ancestry in Arabia. His mother traced her lineage to the prophet Muhammed. His full name, Raham Abdul Arafat al-Qudwa al-Hussayni, indicates his rich genealogy. "Arafat" was for the sacred mountain near Mecca where Muhammed supposedly got his first message from Allah. "Yasser" was given to him by his teacher in honor of a Palestinian resistance leader.

A moody boy with hypnotic eyes that could stop a stranger in mid-sentence, Arafat was schooled in the resistance movement against Zionist immigrants and British bosses. His father was active in a branch of the fanatical Muslim Brotherhood sect which wanted an Islamic kingdom in Palestine. His teacher, Majid Halaby, a Lebanese Muslim with a Christian background, was a fervent Arab nationalist with a longstanding hatred for colonialism. Both father and teacher tutored young Yasser in guerrilla warfare.

At sixteen Arafat organized his schoolmates into a cell of saboteurs. He lectured anyone who would listen about the illegality of both the British mandate and Zionist immigration. He compared the Palestinian resistance to the Arab fight against the Crusaders.

The resistance movement took arms from the Axis during World War II. German and Italian diplomats promised an independent Palestine if they would help defeat the British. When the Allies won, this hope was dashed.

The victory of Israel in 1948 was a greater blow, but it did not end the resistance. In 1949 Arafat enrolled at King Fuad University in Cairo and helped organize a student federation to fight for an Arab state in Palestine. Arafat's major was civil engineering. He wanted to learn all he could about explosives.

Details of his university days are murky. It is certain that he and his friends were impatient with national leadership in the Arab world. They were angry at Jordan's King Abdullah for allowing British troops to remain in his country, for annexing land on the West Bank of the Jordan River which the Jews had not taken in 1948, and for negotiating with Israel on various matters. They cheered when agents of the fanatical Brotherhood assassinated Abdullah while his fifteen-year-old grandson, Hussein, looked on. Abdullah was succeeded by his son Talal who had to be deposed by the Jordanian parliament because of mental illness. Young Hussein came to the throne in 1953 and has survived to this day.

They further cheered the removal of King Farouk of ·Egypt, an obese playboy whose main interests were food and women. Their idol became Gamal Nasser who made himself dictator of Egypt in 1954.

Nasser played on the passions of the Palestinians and promised to finance a guerrilla army. Arafat joined up and went on several raids into Israel. His skills in planting explosives came in handy.

They applauded Nasser in 1956 when he accepted Russian aid after the U.S. cut off support for his Aswan Dam project. They acclaimed the Egyptian dictator for nationalizing the Suez Canal from its British and French owners and stopping Israeli ships at the Gulf of Aqaba. When Israel invaded the Sinai and the Gaza Strip in retaliation, they fought side by side with Egyptians.

The Egyptians fell back in panic. In one company of forty men, only Arafat and two others stood their ground. "This," he says today, "was when I lost my faith in the Egyptians' ability to defeat Israel."

Arafat and the Palestinians realized they would have to lead the fight for their land. He and three close friends started a construction business in Kuwait to finance the revolution. Here they organized Al Fatah—derived from an acronym from Arabic words *Harakat al Tahrir al-Falastin* meaning, "Movement for the Liberation of Palestine." The initials are reversed to FTH, pronounced "faht," meaning "conquest," hence Fatah. Fatah soon became the largest of the Palestinian *fedayeen* groups.

Arafat started a magazine *Our Palestine* which he hoped would stir up volunteers among the Palestinian refugees. When the response was slow, he toured the camps in 1961. The "degradation and humiliation," which he saw, "convinced me that the Jews were doing to my people what the Nazis had done to them. Correcting the situation became all that mattered to me."

Algerian nationalists won independence from France the next year. Arafat and other Fatah leaders went to Algiers to learn how the Algerians had done it. Ben Bella, the Algerian leader, set them up an office where Palestinians could come from anywhere and get diplomatic papers to work in the Arab world. They would have to assign a large percentage of their salaries for the Palestinian cause.

Arafat had an organization and means for support. Now he had to persuade the Arab masses that Israel could be defeated. The Arab leaders did not want another war. They had too many internal problems of their own to contend with at the moment.

An opportunity fell into his lap when Israel suddenly disclosed the damming of the upper Jordan and diversion of much of the water through a canal for irrigation of the dry Negev desert. The news hit Arab capitals like a thunderbolt. Arab leaders wailed that it was illegal and predicted the diversion would dry up the crops in Jordanian territory along the lower river.

While Arab heads of state fumed, Arafat set up a cunning propaganda trap to goad them into another war. In his magazine he told the story about a group of mice that agreed to hang a bell on a hungry cat that wanted to eat them. But no mouse was willing to bell the cat. "The situation is the reverse today," Arafat said. "We have thirteen cats in the Arab League and not one will hang the bell on the Zionist mouse."

Nasser was infuriated and tried to bell Fatah and other troublesome Palestinian groups. He proposed that the Arab League set up the Palestine Liberation Organization as an umbrella over all the groups, including Fatah. All the Arab countries jumped at this, except Syria which was feuding with Egypt. Many of the contributors to Fatah now began giving to the PLO.

Arafat got Syria to sponsor Fatah. With Syrian aid, a Fatah cadre was dispatched to blow up the water diversion canal while Arafat and others flew to Beirut and dropped copies of Fatah's Military Communique No. 1 into newspaper mailboxes. The saboteurs botched the canal job, but Arafat's story on "the opening shot in the Palestinian Revolution" appeared on the front pages.

More raids and communiques followed. To the Arab masses it appeared that Fatah was belling the Zionists. Israel was not seriously hurt, but the Arab leaders were put on the defensive. To criticize Arafat and the Fatah meant risking retaliation, perhaps even a revolt from hotheads in their own governments.

Fatah moved into Jordan without permission and opened attack bases on the West Bank near refugee camps. Young King Hussein protested to the Syrians.

They did nothing—all while Fatah recruiters canvassed the camps, recruiting more guerrillas, and sending them out on suicide raids.

Suddenly the Syrian government was toppled by a coup. The new leaders tried to clamp down on Fatah's terrorism. Then Nasser tried to show up both Syria and Fatah by launching guerrilla attacks on Israel from Egypt. The new Syrian government now felt it had to endorse terrorism against Israel.

In a game of "who's afraid of Israel?" Syria dared Nasser into demanding the removal of the UN buffer force that had been in the Sinai since the 1956 war. On June 4, 1967, Cairo radio crowed, "We will wipe Israel off the face of the map and no Jew will remain alive." Fearing an imminent attack from her hostile neighbors, Israel struck at Egypt, Jordan, and Syria. Outnumbered more than two to one in soldiers and equipment, the Israelis tripled their territory in six swift days. They retook the Sinai, the Gaza Strip, and added the strategic Golan Heights and the West Bank of the Jordan, which included east Jerusalem where the Temple site was located. Jews ran through the narrow streets to the historic Wailing Wall and shouted prayers of gratitude while the Arabs licked the wounds from their worst defeat ever.

The only Arab victors were Arafat and his Fatah who had sat out the war in refugee camps in Lebanon. When the war ended, they were on the move with press releases and weapons. Day after day the Arab world heard about the exploits of Fatah. The voices of moderate Palestinians and other Arabs who abhorred the killing of innocent civilians went unheard. Fatah guerrillas were the men of the hour and Arafat was their Saladin leading the holy war to drive the invaders out.

As Arafat had anticipated, foreign journalists and TV

crews swarmed into Fatah bases. Arafat, wearing his black and white checkered *kaffiyeh* and pistol on his side, was prime-time interview material. After seeing him, they were then given a tour of refugee camps by Fatah escorts for first-hand observation of the suffering Palestinians.

Arafat had never taken orders from PLO officials. Now, because of the prominence of Fatah, he took over the top job of chairman. Under his leadership the PLO became in effect a government-in-exile. The Soviet Union, China, and many smaller nations endorsed the PLO as the "legitimate" government of the displaced Palestinians.

Fatah now opened bases in Jordan, embarrassing King Hussein. The most moderate of the Arab leaders, Hussein wanted a permanent peace with Israel. Jordan had lost the West Bank to Israel in the Six-Day War. Jordan had no oil wells, little industry, and 800,000 Palestinian refugees who existed on a UN starvation diet. Israeli retaliatory raids against the Fatah guerrillas in Jordanian territory were making the economy worse and keeping the country in turmoil.

Hussein finally had enough. He struck an agreement with Israel on August 6, 1970. The Israelis pledged to stop their raids into Jordan. Hussein would keep Fatah at bay. To enforce the pact, Jordanian soldiers took up positions around Fatah's camps.

On September 1 Hussein narrowly escaped an assassination attempt. Five days later Palestinians more radical than Arafat grabbed world headlines by hijacking four jet airliners over Europe and diverting three planes to the Middle East. They took 150 passengers as hostages and destroyed a Pan Am 747 on a desert landing strip.

Reacting swiftly, Hussein's soldiers hit Fatah's bases

and killed scores of guerrillas. The country almost erupted into full-scale civil war before outside Arab leaders arranged a truce. Fatah survivors joined comrades in and around the refugee camps of southern Lebanon. This area soon became known as Fatah land.

Hussein's government kept trying for a settlement with Israel which Fatah and other guerrilla groups fanatically opposed. On November 19, 1971, Palestinian assassins gunned down the Jordanian prime minister in Cairo. Undaunted, Hussein proposed that Palestinians on both the East Bank and the Israeli-occupied West Bank of the Jordan River form an autonomous state federated with Jordan. The plan was immediately rejected by Israel and condemned, under PLO influence, by Syria and Egypt.

Fatah and the more extreme guerrilla groups kept up the pressure. On May 30, 1972, one group hit the Tel Aviv airport, killing twenty-six people and wounding seventy-nine others. Three weeks later Israeli planes bombed Palestinian refugee camps in Lebanon, killing twenty-four.

The tit-for-tat responses continued. On September 5 the "Black September" band (named for the month when Hussein drove guerrillas out of Jordan) shocked the world by killing eleven Israeli athletes at the Munich Olympics. Israel responded with heavy bombing and troop raids in southern Lebanon.

The following March another Palestinian group cut down three prominent diplomats, two of them Americans, in Sudan. Israeli commandos slipped into Beirut and killed three PLO leaders in reprisal.

The guerrillas had both the Arab nations and Israel in a bind. The Arab countries refused to recognize Israel's right to exist because Israel refused to withdraw from

165

territories occupied in the 1967 war. And Israel refused to withdraw because her Arab neighbors would not guarantee her survival.

The thin ice broke again in the fall of 1973 when Syria and Egypt attacked Israel on Yom Kippur, the holiest day of the Jewish year. The Arabs were advancing on both fronts when an American airlift of arms put the Israelis on the offensive. One Israeli force was nearing Damascus and another was deep into Egypt when the U.S. and Russia enforced a cease-fire. The two superpowers had been close to nuclear war.

Yom Kippur was followed by the devastating Arab oil boycott on the U.S. and other countries that had supported Israel. It was the only way the Arabs had of getting back at the West.

Arafat's star kept ascending. In 1974 he was invited to address the United Nations General Assembly, the only head of a nonexistent nation ever so honored.

This was a far different UN from 1947 when the U.S. controlled a majority of votes. The Third World of Arab, African, and Asian nations now held the reins, and most backed the PLO's fight for a Palestinian state.

Jews demonstrated every day in New York the week before his arrival. They carried such signs as, "UN STANDS FOR UNITED TERROR" and "HAS THE UN SOLD OUT JUSTICE FOR POLITICS?" The "operations officer" of the radical Jewish Defense League was arrested on a charge of threatening to kill Arafat. A thousand policemen were required to provide for the PLO leader's security.

Arafat was also the only speaker ever to address the UN wearing a gun. Aides claimed it was unloaded.

When Arafat was introduced, the Israeli diplomats walked out. "I am a rebel, and freedom is my cause," he declared to a rousing ovation.

He called the Israelis "foreign invaders" and accused them of destroying nineteen thousand Arab houses in trying to punish dissenters during the past seven years.

"The root of our cause," he asserted, "is represented by those . . . who, while they occupy our homes, as their cattle graze in our pastures and as their hands pluck the fruit from our trees, claim . . . that we are disembodied spirits, fictions without presence, without traditions or future."

He proposed that Palestine be re-created a secular democratic state in which Christians, Jews, and Muslims would have equal rights. "The Jews of Europe and the U.S. have been known to lead the struggles for secularism and the separation of church and state; they have also been known to fight against discrimination on religious grounds," he said. "How do they then refuse this humane paradigm for the Holy Land?"

He concluded with a dramatic touch. "I have come bearing an olive branch and a freedom fighter's gun. Do not let the olive branch fall from my hand." Then clasping hands over head in a victory symbol, he departed amidst waves of applause.

Israel was predictably outraged. Israeli ambassador Yosef Tekoah accused the UN of "prostrating" itself before the PLO "which stands for the premeditated murder of innocent civilians, denies to the Jewish people its right to live and seeks to destroy the Jewish state by armed force." One Israeli newspaper termed Arafat's speech "the voice of naked terrorism."

Then, as if Arafat's UN speech were not blow enough, the UN passed a resolution classifying Zionism as "racism." Israel protested mightily. Many American political leaders condemned the UN. But the resolution was not rescinded.

It can be argued that Arafat is no worse than Menachem Begin when he was the commander of the Irgun. Begin once said, "Our enemies called us terrorists, our friends patriots." Begin was asked in February 1978 by CBS-TV's Mike Wallace if he saw any difference in what he did as leader of the Irgun from Arafat's actions. Begin frowned and began talking about the horrors of the Nazi Holocaust. Wallace, in later comment, quoted a political opponent of Begin: "He considers himself an instrument of history. He doesn't see right or wrong." The same may be said of Arafat.

Does Arafat represent the majority of the Palestinians? No hard statistics are available to indicate the extent of his following, although he is the dominant leader of the fight for a Palestinian state. Does the majority agree with his tactics of terrorism and unswerving militancy against Israel? Many knowledgeable observers think there are thousands of responsible Palestinians who are opposed to Arafat and are horrified by the indiscriminate killing. However, they are intimidated by guerrilla death threats against anyone who proposes to "compromise" with Israel.

These observers, who include Christian missionaries, add that Arafat and the guerrillas would have no appeal and power if certain conditions did not exist. They cite the now over two million refugees outside Israel and its occupied territories, and systematic discrimination and harassment against Palestinians inside the occupied lands by Israeli soldiers. Palestinian property, they say, is taken by Israeli settlers without payment; houses are blown up or sealed off in villages where suspected guerrillas have been seen; deep wells are dug that divert precious water from neighboring Palestinian farms; and guerrilla suspects are imprisoned and tortured without regard to basic human rights. A Swiss League for Human Rights observation mission concluded following a visit to the West Bank in 1977 that Israeli officials and soldiers were guilty of "repeated violation of the provisions of the Universal Declaration of Human Rights."

Against all this, Anwar Sadat made his "sacred mission" to Jerusalem, offering peace and calling for Israeli withdrawal from occupied lands and self-determination for the Palestinians. No other Arab leader joined the peace talks, not even Hussein. Hard-line Arab countries hurled diatribes across the radio airways. "Listen, O Sadat," shouted Damascus radio, "Syria, the Arab, comes out to declare its huge anger. . . . Syria stands in the face of conspiracies. Syria refuses defeat."

The PLO called Sadat a Judas to the Arab cause. Declared Salah Khalaf, the number two man in Fatah after Arafat, "Sadat has nothing to do with Palestine and no party is entitled to represent the Palestinians except the PLO." He hinted at the possibility of assassination. "Anything planned and agreed on above the heads of the Palestinian people can be abrogated by a single bullet."

Two months later, in February 1978, one of Sadat's closest friends, Youssef Sebai, was killed by Palestinian assassins in Cyprus. Sebai was the editor of a major Cairo newspaper and Egypt's most respected journalist. Ten Egyptian soldiers died in an attempt to rescue hostages from the Palestinians.

To make matters worse, Begin announced a new interpretation of UN Resolution 242 that calls for withdrawal from occupied territories. The West Bank, he said, was not occupied but "liberated" territory. It belonged to Israel by divine right and was also essential for the defense of Israel. Israeli settlements there were perfectly legal.

Begin's hard-line stance gave the peace talks a grave setback and deflated Sadat even more in the eyes of Arab neighbors.

Then in March came the daring Fatah attack on an Israeli tour bus near Tel Aviv. They stopped the bus, shouting, "Palestine! Arafat! Liberation from the Zionists!" When the carnage was done, thirty-six Israelis and nine guerrillas were dead and seventy-two other persons wounded. Many of the dead were children.

The Israelis retaliated with their greatest attack against the Palestinians ever. Vowing to "sever the arm of iniquity," ten thousand Jewish soldiers, backed up by bombers and missile-armed boats, smashed deep into southern Lebanon. Operation "Stone of Wisdom," as it was called, resulted in the loss of only about twenty Israelis. From three hundred to a thousand guerrillas, refugees, and Lebanese were killed and some 160,000 Lebanese left homeless. The casualty count pulled the Israelis way ahead of their enemy; since the 1973 war, Palestinian *fedayeen* had killed 143 Israelis, while Israeli retaliatory strikes had accounted for around two thousand Arab deaths.

The UN acted quickly on the new crisis and sent buffer troops to the area. But the Fatah attack and the devastating Israeli reprisal had, in the view of most diplomats, all but wiped out Sadat's "sacred mission" for peace.

Begin now went ahead with a planned trip to Washington. He met a stern U.S. president. Jimmy Carter suggested Israel might have overreacted in the strike into Lebanon. Carter also noted that peace had previously been pursued "under the broad scope of UN Resolution 242." Israel should give up occupied territory, including the West Bank, in exchange for U.S. guarantee of her security. Begin was unyielding.

"Taking [his] case to the American people," Begin reiterated before the National Press Club in Washington that Jews had "the perfect right . . . to settle in the land of their forefathers." The press comment that followed was decidedly unfriendly. Said columnist Carl Rowan, "Begin seems not to understand that everyone has forefathers, but they don't have the right to seize and settle on whatever they declare to be the land of their forefathers."

Begin got a much friendlier reaction from Rabbi Alexander Schindler, chairman of the Conference of Presidents of Major American Jewish Organizations. The month before the Conference had issued a statement, labeling the position of "Anwar Sadat, Superstar" as "hard-line" and "obstinate." Rabbi Schindler now called Begin a "worthy leader not only in Israel but of the entire Jewish people."

Begin actually irritated many American Jews, but few spoke out. The reason, *New York Times* liberal columnist Anthony Lewis explained, was that they were afraid criticism of Begin's hard line might be interpreted as disloyalty to the cause of Israel.

So the peace talks are snagged by the troublesome Palestinians and the intransigent Begin. Sadat, who has said he will resign if his mission fails, has put himself on a shaky limb.

Should Sadat resign, or even worse, be assassinated, Egypt would be left with a vacuum in leadership. A hard-line dictator could take over, unfriendly to the West, and eager for war with Israel. Other "moderate" Arab nations might join a common front. With arms purchased from oil revenues, the Arabs might attack again.

To push this dread scenario further: The U.S. would

probably go to Israel's aid. The Arab oil countries would call another oil boycott. Radical Arabs might even move on the oil fields.

The U.S. would protect her vital interests. The Soviets would back the Arabs. World War III. Nuclear disaster. Hundreds of millions killed.

Impossible?

Yasser Arafat said before the 1976 U.S. presidential election, "Each time you Americans deny the Palestinians their just due, you come closer to your own holocaust."

Jimmy Carter said soon after his election that the Palestinians should have a "homeland." No American president ever said that before. Carter has since said that he did not mean an independent Palestinian state, certainly not one governed by the PLO.

This qualification has not satisfied the American Jewish establishment. Political analysts say if a new election were held today, Jews who traditionally vote Democratic would turn against Carter. They would undoubtedly have the backing of millions of American Christians who hold that Israel must hang on to the West Bank (Samaria and Judea) because of their belief that Bible prophecy assigns it to "God's chosen people," the Jews.

Where does this leave the Palestinians, many of whom are professing Christians? They and many others are asking, "Is God against the Palestinians and for Israel?"

10

Whose Side Is God On?

Twelve days after the Six-Day War ended, Soviet Premier Aleksei Kosygin and U.S. President Lyndon Johnson met for summit talks in the quiet college town of Glassboro, New Jersey. Kosygin wanted Israel to give up conquered territory. Johnson declined to press Israel on the matter.

Kosygin frowned. "I don't understand you Americans backing Israel. There are 80 million Arabs* and only 3 million Israelis. It doesn't make sense. Why do it?"

"Because it's right," Johnson said.

Right or wrong, America has been Israel's staunchest friend and protector since 1948. Undoubtedly, without this "special relationship," endorsed by every president and Congress during the past thirty years, Israel would not today exist.

The numbers make this friendship plain. In 1948 before

---

* Kosygin's numbers were off. The population of the Arab countries was then 110 million.

Israel declared statehood, a poll showed 80 per cent of Americans backing the Zionist program. In 1967 at the time of the Six-Day War another poll showed 96 per cent of Americans supporting Israel.

Aid figures are equally impressive. Since 1973, for example, $10 billion in U.S. aid, half in military equipment, has gone to the Israelis. In 1977 Israel received $1.4 billion, more than one-fifth of the total U.S. aid programs to all nations. This does not include private aid. From 1948-68 alone the United Jewish Appeal raised over $4 billion for Israel. In 1974 the UJA collected almost $1 billion in a single year.

Israel's power in American politics is formidable. A majority of U.S. representatives and senators have backed Israel on all major issues since 1948. For example, after Arafat addressed the UN, seventy-one senators sent a public letter to President Ford, urging firm support of Israel and rejection of the PLO.

High officials, who dare speak critically of Israel, quickly feel the heat. General George S. Brown, chairman of the Joint Chiefs of Staff, was pounded for suggesting in 1974 that a[Jewish] propaganda group had pushed the American government to support Israel. "Racist and clearly anti-Semitic," said one of many protesting letter writers to *Time* which had quoted his remarks.

In 1978 Zbigniew Brzezinski, security adviser to President Jimmy Carter, was raked for his position that Israel should return territories occupied in the Six-Day War. Brzezinski called the attacks "a subtle kind of pressure. If you don't agree with us, they are saying, we're going to stamp you an anti-Semite." Brzezinski is probably secure in his appointive position, but few American politicians can win elections while being accused of anti-Semitism. Ask John Conlan of Arizona, who generally supported Israel while in Congress. Running for the Senate in 1976, Conlan, an evangelical Christian lay leader, was accused of anti-Semitism by some supporters of his opponent during the last days of the Republican primary. Conlan vigorously denied the charge. The chief rabbi of Phoenix endorsed him. But political analysts agree that it was probably the cause of his narrow loss.

From where then does Israel's power in foreign policy stem? We can only come back to Lyndon Johnson's answer to Kosygin. Most Americans believe it is "right" to favor Israel against her Arab opponents, particularly the PLO.

Reasons for this are not hard to deduce. A strong residual of sympathy continues for survivors of the Nazi Holocaust and other Jewish refugees from European persecution. Americans have sympathized with Jews trying to emigrate from Soviet Russia where they have been persecuted for decades. Thousands of American Jews have relatives in Israel. Israel, it is often said, "is the most democratic country in the Middle East." Israel is also admired for its commitment to the work ethic, a belief etched in the American heritage. And Israel is seen as the underdog against the Arabs, even though she has received the most advanced military equipment in the world, short of nuclear missiles and bombs, from her U.S. ally.

Still we have not come to the strongest factor in American life for Israel's rightness, something that went largely unnoticed by the big media before 1970. This is the conviction held by a third or more American Protestant evangelicals that modern Israel is a direct fulfillment of biblical prophecy and the most important sign in over nineteen hundred years that the Second Coming of Christ is near.

Hundreds of books have been written on this subject, but before 1970 none reached the mass market. That year a small 180-page volume called *The Late Great Planet Earth* hit like a spectacular meteor from outer space. Described as "Amazing Biblical Prophecies About This Generation!" it was written by Hal Lindsey, a converted Mississippi river boat captain, then an evangelist for the fast-growing Campus Crusade for Christ International. The Lindsey book set the mass communications industry abuzz. Within eight years *The Late Great Planet Earth* and five other Lindsey books would sell over 14 million copies.

Said Lindsey in his first book: "With the Jewish nation reborn in the land of Palestine, ancient Jerusalem once again under total Jewish control for the first time in 2600 years, and talk of rebuilding the great Temple . . . this has now set the stage for the other predicted signs to develop in history. It [Israel] is like the key piece of a jigsaw puzzle being found and then having the many adjacent pieces rapidly fall into place."

Lindsey grabbed the attention of millions outside the evangelical pale, although he said nothing that hadn't been said in earlier books of prophecy. It was the way he wrote of Israel fulfilling prophecy in 1948 and 1967 and of startling events to follow. Suddenly the frightening drift of the world began to make sense.

Lindsey followed a system of biblical interpretation and chronology known as dispensationalism. Dispensationalists divide the whole of time from creation to the final judgment into seven time periods: *innocence*—from the creation of man to the Fall in Eden, *conscience*—from the Fall to the Noahic flood, *human government*—from the great flood to Abraham's call in Mesopotamia, *promise*—from the call to the giving of the Mosaic law, *law*—from Sinai to the crucifixion of Christ, *grace*—from the death of Christ to the consummation of the Gentile age when the last of God's elect is evangelized, and the *kingdom* age or dispensation which begins with Christ's reign over a peaceful earth for a thousand years, and climaxes with the final judgments, the banishment of Satan and his hordes, and the eternal new heavens and new earth. Because dispensationalists believe Christ will return before the millennium, they are also premillennialists, in contrast to amillennialists who believe the thousand years specified in Revelation 20 is symbolic, and postmillennialists who think Christ will return at the end of a thousand years of righteousness.

Dispensationalists in the last half of the nineteenth century were more confident of a Jewish state in Palestine than Jews. Charles C. Ryrie, Dean of the Graduate School, Dallas Theological Seminary (dispensationalism's most highly regarded theological school), wrote in his book, *The Bible and Tomorrow's News*: ". . . As late as the nineteenth century, their loss of Palestine was accepted by many Jews, and the idea of their ever returning was kept alive more by premillennial Christians than anyone else. Then . . . persecution of Jews in Russia and Germany forced many Jews to think of setting up a colony of Jews in Palestine."

When it appeared that statehood for Israel, the *first stage* in the dispensational prophetic timetable, was close, dispensationalists became highly confident. T. DeCourcy Rayner, a leading Israel-watcher among Canadian dispensationalists, wrote in 1947 when the "partition" controversy was raging at the UN: ". . . The Jews will eventually be given not a partitioned Palestine, but the whole of the land, and ultimately the whole of Transjordan as well. This may sound fantastic, yet I dare to assert it on the authority of One who cannot lie, and whose revealed Word can never fail." Rayner's article was published in *Moody Monthly*, the official organ of Moody Bible Institute, the "queen" of the dispensational Bible colleges.

The *second stage* in the dispensational end-times scenario is Jewish repossession of the sacred Temple site in Jerusalem. This accomplishment in the Six-Day War in 1967 gave dispensationalists much wider credibility.

The *third stage* is the rebuilding of the Temple and reinstitution of the Levitical sacrifice system on the site now occupied by Islam's Dome of the Rock. Dispensationalists believe this could happen very soon. They concede that Muslims are unlikely to voluntarily relocate their holy place. Hal Lindsey thinks an earthquake might solve the problem. "Obstacle or no obstacle," he insists, "the Temple will be rebuilt. Prophecy demands it."

Every rumor on rebuilding the Temple is received with great excitement in the dispensational camp. One story started from a tourist hearing in Italy that marble was being mined for "the Temple." She told her pastor and he passed it on to a magazine. Other periodicals copied the story. Hundreds of preachers used it in sermons. Then it was learned that the marble was for a new Reformed Jewish temple in an Italian city.

Other stories circulate of large sums of money being solicited among Jews and dispensational Christians and of loads of marble being sent to Israel for the Temple rebuilding. Rabbi Nathan H. Zwitman is known to have been in Miami raising funds for the project. Tourists at the Temple site have observed excavations. They were told workers were searching for the long lost Ark of the Covenant, which would be housed in a new temple.

The *fourth stage* will be the secret Second Coming of Christ for His church, which dispensationalists call the "Rapture." Believers will be "snatched" away in the greatest mass disappearance of people in history. This will mark the end of the "church age."

The *fifth stage* will be the rise of a confederation of ten European nations from the old Roman Empire, which some believe will include the United States. This alliance will probably begin forming before the Rapture. The European Common Market is proposed by Lindsey and others as a precursor of this confederation.

The "prince" over these nations will make a covenant with Israel, guaranteeing freedom to continue the sacrifices at the new Temple. This one, who could be alive now, is the Antichrist of the Bible. Numerous Antichrist candidates have been suggested through the centuries. Luther and Calvin identified him with the papacy. Later, Protestants thought he was Napoleon. Mussolini and Hitler were strong contenders in this century. More recently, Henry Kissinger has received the "honor." Numerologists noted that his name came to 111, when letters were numbered in the order of A-1, B-2, C-3, etc., and added together. They multiplied this figure by six, the biblical number for man by virtue of being created on the sixth day, and got 666, the mystery number given in Revelation 13:18.

Dispensational scholars frown on such guessing games. But they are convinced the Antichrist will make a covenant with Israel and then doublecross the Israeli government by moving into the Temple and proclaiming himself God. From there he will order his subjects to receive a mark in their right hand or forehead as proof of their loyalty to him. Those without this mark cannot buy or sell. Some prophecy writers are warning that the universal metric system and electronic grocery check-outs are signs of the coming of this great controller.

The *sixth stage* will be marked by a series of wars and a "Great Tribulation" of seven years leading up to the final battle of Armageddon. The Antichrist, say many dispensationalists, will be caught between two great alliances. Egypt will lead a coalition of Arab and black African nations on Jerusalem from the south. The Soviet Union will lead another group down from the far north. They will join forces with the southern powers and encircle Jerusalem. The Soviets will betray the Arabs. China will intervene against the Soviets and send in 200 million soldiers to fight them and their allies. When the terrible war is over, the Antichrist will emerge on top and begin a purge. During this "Great Tribulation" anyone caught without the "mark of the beast" will be killed.

At this time, when it appears that evil has triumphed, Christ will return to earth in "great glory" with His saints. In the final battle of Armageddon between good and evil, His forces will defeat the Antichrist and his armies. At this time (or just before Christ returns with His people) one-third or more of the Jews will accept Jesus as their Messiah.

The *seventh stage* will be the millennium, spoken of in Revelation 20. Satan will be bound a thousand years "that he should deceive the nations no more" (v. 3). Christ will reign from Jerusalem over a renewed and peaceful earth.

At the end of the millennium, Satan will be "loosed[for] a little season" (Revelation 20:3). After failing in a final effort to overthrow Christ, he will be cast into the eternal lake of fire.

The *eighth and final stage* will mark the climax of

history. The final judgments will occur. Sinners will be consigned to hell and punished according to their works. The old order will pass away and true believers will live with God forever in the new heavens and the new earth.

The preceding outline generally represents the dispensational interpretation of the end times. Supporting passages are gathered principally from Jeremiah, Ezekiel, Daniel, Zechariah, Matthew 24 and 25, and Revelation. Because of the collation and juxtaposition of so many passages, the timetables drawn from Daniel and Revelation, and the difficulty of deciding which Scriptures are symbolic and which are not, interpreters disagree at many points.

Some differ over the time of Christ's return in relation to the Great Tribulation under Antichrist. "Pre-tribs" say Christ will return for His church just before the Great Tribulation. "Mid-tribbers" say the event will occur at the half-way point. "Post-tribbers" say believers alive at that time will have to endure and wait for Christ's return until the end of the Tribulation. The majority of present dispensationalists hold the pre-trib position, which is certainly the most comforting to contemplate.

Differences over the character of restored Israel is more relevant to the Middle East conflict today. Hal Lindsey and most dispensationalists hold that the present nation of Israel is fulfillment of prophecy. That the founding Zionists were not particularly religious and that Israel is basically a secular state does not bother them. The spiritual restoration will come in due time they say.

A minority of dispensationalists believe a substantial remnant of Jews must be converted to Christ before the return to Palestine can be validated. This view is seldom heard today, but it was prominent in the 1930s and '40s.

Israel's "hope is to be gathered back to their own land,

and established there with their Messiah in their midst,"
wrote William R. Newell, a long-time teacher at the
Moody Bible Institute, in 1938. Shortly after Israel
became a state, Henry Jacobsen, the adult editor of
Scripture Press Publications, a Sunday school publisher
for thousands of dispensational churches, said, "Many
Jews believe that their destiny is wrapped up with
modern political Israel, which has grown out of the Zionist
movement. . . . No one can flatly deny that there is any
connection between Zionism, Israel, and the *eventual*
restoration of the Jews; we can be sure, however, that
these present-day movements will not produce the
restoration of which the New Testament speaks, for that
time of blessing will come only when the Jews look on Him
whom they pierced."

Some missionaries in Palestine before 1948 held to a
spiritual restoration. William F. Smalley, the senior
worker for the respected Christian and Missionary
Alliance, wrote in 1935, "The purpose of the present
movement among Jews is national restoration. But the
ultimate aim of Jehovah . . . is vastly different. God has
in view not national restoration, but national conversion;
not the settling of them in Palestine to become one of the
nations. . . ." In 1937 Smalley thought there might be "an
independent Jewish State within the next few months.
. . . Yet how disappointing! Zionists' ambitions are being
fulfilled without Zion."

Some Orthodox Jews living in Palestine then thought
the Zionists' political plan blasphemy. They insisted there
could be no state of Israel until the messiah (not Jesus)
appeared. This group, known as Kartas, said the Nazi
slaughter of Jews was God's punishment for premature
settling in Palestine. They refused to recognize Israeli
statehood in 1948. After the 1967 war, they went into

virtual mourning and flew black flags from their housetops. The Kartas still refuse to pay taxes and to handle currency with pictures of Zionist founders. Some met secretly with Yasser Arafat, when the PLO leader visited the UN in 1974.

Since Sadat's dramatic call for peace, many dispensationalists have been reassessing Egypt's role in events to come. Some call Sadat's peace ploy a tool of Satan. Some say a remnant of Egyptians will be converted to Christianity. Some say Egypt will not be part of the alliance of the south that will attack Israel.

William Malgo, author of a recent paperback, *Begin with Sadat*, and a fervent backer of Israel, takes the latter position. Syria, he forecasts, will join up with the Antichrist. Egypt, he explains, is from Ishmael and the beneficiaries of Abraham's promise, while the Syrians are from Nahor, Abraham's unbelieving brother.

Malgo warns, however, that Egypt's blessings will depend on her support of Israel. "History clearly tells us that as long as Egypt blessed Israel, it also was blessed and as soon as it persecuted or cursed Israel, it was persecuted and cursed also." Malgo praises Israel's Begin. "He loves God, he believes the Bible, and he takes God's oath seriously."

The new appraisals of Egypt should not be taken to mean that Christian dispensationalists are likely to give up their belief that Jews are God's chosen, covenant people, who continue as beneficiaries of biblical prophecies. As Herbert Lockyer, author of over fifty religious books, puts it, "When it comes to prophecy, the Jew is ever God's index finger, and all belonging to the Jew will yet be realized."

The dispensational scenario for Israel is held so strongly that many adherents believe it is the only biblical prospectus for the future. Author Alan Taylor quotes a Dutch theologian as saying, "If Israel were to cease to exist as an independent Jewish state, I don't know whether I could continue to believe in God."

Actually, dispensationalism, as taught today, is little more than a century old. Throughout most of Christian history, Protestant and Catholic theologians tended to believe that the Old Testament promises to the Jews were consummated in Christ and the Church in which there is no separation between races and nationalities and all believers are children of Abraham by faith.

Dispensationalists readily admit this, but claim that their end-times theology is a return to the teachings of the earliest Church fathers.

Many Christian leaders of the second and third centuries did expect Christ to suddenly return and reign from Jerusalem for a thousand years before the final judgment and the new heavens and new earth. Said Justin Martyr (A.D. 100-165): "I and others, who are right-minded Christians at all points, are assured that there will be a resurrection of the dead, and a thousand years in Jerusalem, which will then be built, adorned, and enlarged as the prophets Ezekiel and Isaiah and others declare." The thousand years came from Revelation 20 and a teaching of Judaism that allegorized the six days of creation into six millenniums of history, to be followed by a thousand-year day of spiritual rest. They took their text from Psalm 90:4: "One day with the Lord is as a thousand years, and a thousand years as one day." But they never developed a prophetic timetable such as modern dispensationalists follow.

The early millennial idea soon degenerated into a material paradise. Jerome (347-420) spoke disapprovingly of "these half-Jews who look for a Jerusalem of gold and precious stones from heaven, and a future kingdom of a thousand years, in which all nations shall serve Israel." Augustine (354-430) finally dealt the belief a staggering blow. At one time a millenarian, he became convinced that apocalyptic passages in Daniel, Ezekiel, and Revelation should be taken spiritually and symbolically to refer to God's ultimate victory over evil and the triumph of Christ and His Church.

Augustinianism, a millennial theology, prevailed in the Catholic church. The Protestant reformers also generally followed the Bishop of Hippo.

A variant idea arose among the English Puritans. Daniel Whitby (1638-1721) taught that a millennium must occur before the Second Coming of Christ. Whitby anticipated a powerful outpouring of the Holy Spirit under which the Jews would be converted to Christ, the Turkish sultan be overthrown, and all non-Christian religions and atheistic philosophies be overcome by Christ. The whole world would be brought under the spiritual reign of Christ for a thousand years. Then He would return. Whitby's postmillennial views captivated the evangelical clergy of colonial America and powered missionary thrusts into Asia and Africa. The surge of millennial optimism survived into the early twentieth century. Many of today's best-loved hymns from this period reflect the postmillennial expectation of an outpouring of the Holy Spirit and the bringing in of the kingdom. For example:

The kingdom is coming, O tell ye the story,
God's banner exalted shall be!
The earth shall be full of His knowledge and glory,
As waters that cover the sea.

Modern dispensationalism was born in England among the Plymouth Brethren, a fellowship of independent Christian assemblies that does not hold to a professional clergy. The principal exponent was John Darby.

In 1870 Darby came to Canada and taught at a Bible conference in Ontario. He said that postmillennialism was unscriptural. Instead, the world would worsen, Israel would become a nation again in Palestine, the Antichrist would rise, and then Christ would return for His Church before the Great Tribulation.

One of those he convinced at the conference was Paul Loizeaux, who with his brother Timothy later founded the publishing house that disseminated dispensationalism among American and English Protestants.

The next great figure in dispensationalism was C.I. Scofield, an ex-Confederate soldier, lawyer, and U.S. attorney for Kansas. At forty-six years of age, Scofield "surrendered his life to God" and entered the ministry. He was soon drawn into dispensationalism and began meticulously comparing and cross-referencing Scriptures that appeared to support the view. The Loizeaux brothers greatly admired Scofield and published his first book, *Rightly Dividing the Word of Truth*, which is still in print.

Like Darby, Scofield separated God's dealings with the Church and the nation Israel. Said he in a footnote on Romans 11:1: "The Christian is of the heavenly seed of Abraham, and partakes of the spiritual blessings of the Abrahamic Covenant; but Israel as a nation always has its own place, and is yet to have its greatest exaltation as the earthly people of God."

The Loizeaux brothers and others felt Scofield should prepare an annotated reference Bible. The brothers loaned him their editor, Miss Emily Farmer, to check the notes. After seven more years of work, the *Scofield*

Reference Bible was published in 1909 by the Oxford University Press. It was the first book published by Oxford's American branch and was put on special display in 1978. Millions have been sold and a "revised version" was recently introduced.

It is safe to say that Scofield's notes—which are almost next to Scripture in authority for dispensationalists—have been the single greatest influence in persuading so many evangelical Christians to believe that God is on the side of Israel. This is not just in the West, but wherever missionaries subscribing to dispensationalism have gone.

Many Arab pastors, particularly Baptists, were taught dispensationalism in the first half of the twentieth century. Admits one, "As an Arab I feel for my fellow Arabs and have nationalistic pride, but as a Christian I was taught to accept the Jewish control of Palestine as biblical." Dispensationalism is no longer taught by most missionaries in the Middle East. Says a present Southern Baptist missionary, "I don't believe dispensationalism is scriptural. But if I said so publicly, some of the pastors would wonder if I believed the Bible."

Scofield's annotated Bible was published during a time of great social unrest in America. The scars of Reconstruction, following the Civil War, and political scandals lingered. Millions of new immigrants—mostly European Catholics and Jews—were flooding into great cities, occupying tenements and taxing urban facilities to the limit. Rich "robber baron" capitalists were exploiting the new immigrants and other poor. Labor unrest was mounting. Protestants were frustrated over their inability to evangelize the newcomers, and divided over social ministries to the poor and dispossessed. The postmillennial dream of bringing in the kingdom was fading.

Dispensationalism caught on with Protestant conservatives who opposed church social programs in favor of individual soul-winning. Thousands flocked to prophetic Bible conferences to hear dispensational preachers expound Darby and Scofield's timetables for Scripture. At every conference there was usually at least one sermon on the restoration of Israel to Palestine.

During this same period thousands of conservative Christians left mainline Protestant churches, principally in the North. The Pentecostal schism of the first two decades of the twentieth century was over liberal theology and the lack of spiritual power in the established churches. The fundamentalist breakaway of the 1920s and '30s was largely in protest of liberalism, ecumenical union, and promotion of the social gospel in seminaries. Pentecostals also observed the fundamentalist taboos (no smoking, drinking, dancing, card playing, or theater attendance) and subscribed to the five "fundamentals of the faith": the inspiration and infallibility of Scripture, the deity of Christ, His virgin birth and miracles, His substitutionary death for sinners, and His personal return. However, Pentecostals reacted less strongly to social ministries because of their Wesleyan theology.

Many of the early classic fundamentalist leaders were not dispensationalists. Among them were T. DeWitt Talmage, T.T. Shields, and J. Gresham Machen—still household names in fundamentalism. However, dispensationalism, through prophecy conferences, new Bible schools, and the Scofield Bible, soon came to be understood as the sixth fundamental of the movement.

One further qualification should be made. The fundamentalist and Pentecostal breaches hardly affected Southern church bodies which had split from their

Northern counterparts before the Civil War largely over slavery. They remained isolated and conservative. This is why, for example, that Southern Baptist seminaries were never "taken over" by dispensationalism.

U.S. fundamentalism boomed after World War II in the North and Midwest.

The horrors of war and prospects of a nuclear doomsday had pulled the props from under liberals. Fundamentalists seemed to have the answers. War and other calamities, along with the settling of Jews in Palestine, were signs that the return of Christ was near, they said confidently. Christ alone was the hope of the world and His message should be proclaimed to the ends of the earth.

This was the era of the great Youth for Christ rallies which drew up to seventy-five thousand in major cities. The YFC evangelists brought zip and glamor to Christianity, arousing howls of criticism from mossy church prelates mired in form and tradition. All the YFC preachers carried Scofield Bibles and took many sermons directly from his notes. A young North Carolina preacher named Billy Graham was the first YFC staff evangelist. He was a Southern Baptist but got his dispensational theology at Wheaton College. As his star rose on the world scene, he would keep saying, "Keep your eyes on the Middle East to see prophecy unfolding." Apparently he still holds the belief that the Jews have a special role in the end times. In a 1977 sermon on "The City of the King," he called Jerusalem the "nerve center of the world geographically . . . the salvation center of the world spiritually . . . the storm center of the world prophetically . . . [and] the glory center of the world. . . . Some day it will be the center of peace."

Besides Youth for Christ, there blossomed a whole

network of Bible schools and colleges, radio ministries and Christian stations, Bible conferences, magazines, book publishers, and superchurches. With few exceptions, all believed the state of Israel was a miraculous fulfillment of prophecy. And when Israel recovered the Temple site in 1967 (the second event in the prophetic scenario), excitement was unbounded. An American missionary who was raised in the Middle East and grew up with Palestinian friends in Jerusalem remembers it well. She was on furlough and seated on the platform of a church in Texas when the missionary chairman announced the news that Israel had won. The congregation spontaneously broke into applause and cheers.

She stood to speak but could not control her emotions. For a moment she sobbed uncontrollably, then gathered her faculties and tried to explain the plight of the Palestinians, many of whom were fleeing a second time. "God loves Palestinians, too," she cried. "And so do I. Many of them are Christians." She went on to talk about their suffering and longing to return home. Before she finished, audible sobs could be heard across the auditorium.

Two years later Hal Lindsey delivered *The Late Great Planet Earth* to Zondervan Publishing House.

Lindsey's best seller was written by veteran writer Carole C. Carlson (who had also helped Billy Graham) in crisp newspaper feature language, spiced with dramatic illustrations and predictions, and documented with statistics, dates, and quotes from world leaders. To anyone untutored in theology and biblical linguistics, it was instantly believable. Lindsey later told *Publisher's Weekly*, "If I had been writing fifteen years ago, I wouldn't have had an audience. But a tremendous number of people were beginning to worry about the future, and they were looking everywhere for answers. . . . I'm just part of that phenomenon."

Interest in Israel and the end times has also fueled a boom in films which followed the dispensational view to varying degrees. Billy Graham's organization produced *His Land*. It was praised by dispensationalists but criticized by a Reformed Church official for subtly perpetuating unfair stereotyped images of the Arab while profiling the Israeli in glowing terms.

Hollywood brought out *The Omen*, a dramatization of the demonic powers of the young Antichrist. In 1978 *The Late Great Planet Earth* was released to commercial theaters. Neither bore an evangelical message. In *The Late Great Planet Earth* the Christian Messiah was referred to as "the Prophet Jesus"—an obvious concession to non-Christian viewers.

But there was no hedging about Israel's role in Bible prophecy. Said Lindsey on camera, "The key to the prophetic puzzle is the rebirth of Israel. . . . The Temple will soon be rebuilt on Mount Moriah. . . . The prophecies of the Bible must come true." *Planet Earth* was panned by the respected *Christianity Today* as lacking in "integrity because of its basic presupposition: the world must end within one generation from the birth of the state of Israel. Any opinion of world affairs that does not dovetail with this prophecy is dismissed. . . . Such a voice of despair cannot be the battle cry of the Church. Doomsdayism is blind to the social side of the gospel and the real presence of the Kingdom of God in this age as well as in the next." But this and other criticisms didn't keep the movie from being a box-office hit in many cities.

Through all of these developments, Israel was astonishingly slow in becoming aware of her

191

dispensational allies in America. This was because American Jews dialogued mainly with Protestant clergy in mainline denominations who disdained fundamentalism. After the spate of prophecy publicity following the Six-Day War, Jerusalem woke up and began rolling out the red carpet for visiting preachers and editors.

For example, in 1973, sixteen top editors of the Evangelical Press Association were brought over for the twenty-fifth anniversary of statehood and shown how Israeli citizens had made the desert bloom with productive crops, new housing developments, and factories. Editor Bob Flood of *Moody Monthly* conceded in his report that "our hosts could hardly be expected to show us negatives, or interpret events from an unbiased stance. . . . At the ruins of Jericho we sensed the embarassment of our Jewish guide when he had to explain the abandoned Arab refugee camp just to the north of the Jericho excavation—a sea of dilapidated shacks which mar the landscape. . . ."

Such reservations are rarely expressed and Israel is grateful. Says Professor David Flusser of Hebrew University: "Their[the dispensationalists] reasoning and faith are straightforward and they do not make demands upon us to be moderate, magnanimous or compromising."

The support of American dispensationalists continues unabated. After Jimmy Carter (who said before his election, "Israel is the foundation and fulfillment of biblical prophecy") became the first American president to speak of a Palestinian homeland, three full-page ads appeared in the *New York Times* affirming support of Israel by evangelical friends.*

---

* President Carter sat under both dispensational and nondispensational pastors at his home church in Plains, Georgia. His most influential pastor, the late Reverend Robert Harris, who served the Plains Baptist Church from 1955-67, taught the amillennial view—that spiritual Israel is the Church. For more background on Carter's theological influence see the author's recent book, *The Church That Produced a President* (Wyden Books, N.Y., with distribution by Simon & Schuster).

The first was by the American Board of Missions to the Jews and supported by forty-eight churches. They declared in part: "Because the Jewish people are the people of prophecy, they are the people of the land. And we, knowing Him who made the promise, totally support the people and land of Israel in their God-given, God-promised, God-ordained right to exist. Any person or group of nations opposed to this right isn't just fighting Israel, but God and time itself."

The second, inserted in the November 1, 1977, edition of the *Times* and the *Washington Post*, was titled "Evangelicals' Concern for Israel." Fifteen prominent evangelicals, including the presidents of five seminaries and Wheaton College, affirmed their "belief in the right of Israel to exist" and demonstrated their "grave apprehension concerning the recent direction of American policy vis-a-vis the Middle East." This ad was prepared by Gerald Strober, a Jewish publicist.

Two weeks later, militant fundamentalist Carl McIntire and associates declared in the *Times*, "Fundamentalists Vote with Israel," and endorsed Jewish settlements on the occupied Arab West Bank. This was followed by a "Salute to Israel" rally, sponsored by W.A. Criswell, pastor of the largest church in the Southern Baptist Convention, First Baptist Church of Dallas. The three thousand who attended launched a new organization called "Evangelicals United for Zion."

After all this, it seemed strange that the Israeli parliament would pass an antimissionary law stating that anyone offering "material inducement" to an Israeli to change his religion is liable to a $3,200 fine and five years in prison. And any Israeli converting to a non-Jewish faith for material benefit may go to jail for three years. A woman member of the Knesset Parliament said it was hardly needed since official records showed only seventeen Israeli Jews converting to Christianity from

1974 to 1976. Missionaries in Israel—who work mainly among the Arab population—unanimously denounced the law. The head of the Israeli Secularist League termed it a "charter for persecution." Ironically, the law's passage came just after the Egyptian government had killed a bill proposed by Islamic militants that would make apostasy a capital crime for Muslims.

Jews have always been a priority target of evangelicals who take Romans 1:16 (". . . The gospel of Christ . . . [is] to the Jew first, and also to the Greek") to mean that evangelizing the Jew is the Church's first responsibility. Hundreds of itinerant missionaries have floated in and out of Israel since its founding. Some are believed to be outright frauds, sending false reports home to solicit money from Christians. In 1955 the Christian and Missionary Alliance's Area Director for the Middle East lamented that whenever a Jew is won, "there are numerous missions . . . who immediately compete for the convert, making very attractive offers. . . ." There is no indication that this has changed.

Established U.S. Jewish missions are fervently pro-Israel. The International Board of Jewish Missions flies the Israeli flag beside the American and Christian flags at its headquarters in Chattanooga. Some Hebrew Christian congregations sing the Israeli national anthem at worship services. An evangelist for the Jews for Jesus organization visited Israel in 1977 and was "startled" when "two Arabs appeared by the side of the road. . . . I had forgotten that we would find another people besides the Jews here."

Dissent among fundamentalists over such unqualified backing of Israel has been infrequent. The most noticed challenge in the 1960s came from writer Elisabeth Elliot. Mrs. Elliot had been a heroine in fundamentalist circles since her husband, Jim, and four other missionaries had been killed by Auca Indians in Ecuador in 1956. She had lived with the Indians for a while afterwards and had written two best-selling books, *Through Gates of Splendor* and *Shadow of the Almighty*.

She went to Israel in the fall of 1967 to see if the Israeli victory had resulted in a "new Jerusalem." She was profoundly troubled at what she saw.

"I wanted to know whether Israel was on God's side. Was Israel really for Him? Was there a seeking which made them truly, in Maritain's phrase, 'Pilgrims of the Absolute'? It appeared so, every once in a while.

"At the Wailing Wall, for example, if I had stuck to watching the praying and the earnestness and listened only to the chants and the Shofar, if I hadn't seen the broken houses and the arrogant soldiers and the bewildered, displaced Arabs the picture would have stayed clear and sharp. But the question of justice arose in my mind. . . ."

Mrs. Elliot was also bothered by the question of physical descent of the Jews. She noted that the government of Israel defined a Jew for prospective citizenship as one born of a Jewish mother. What, then, made his mother Jewish?

From study and talking to Jews, she concluded that Jews were in all the racial groups of the world. "It was a shock to me," she wrote, "to realize that it is no more possible to identify a Jew by race than it is a Christian or a Moslem."

Zionism, she concluded, was "a purely political movement with no religious purpose, a point generally overlooked by those who see in it a kind of return to God."

Mrs. Elliot expected that her book would not be warmly received. She declined to acknowledge by name those who gave her assistance. "Some of them would be embarrassed, some of them angered, and some of them endangered if I should mention their names."

More recently, another respected Christian writer took issue with the fifteen prominent evangelicals who signed the November 1, 1977, full-page ad in the *New York Times*. Joseph Bayly, in his column for the monthly *Eternity*, raised five salient points:

1. He objected to the title, "Evangelicals' Concern for Israel." "Who appointed [the signers of the *Times*' ad] as my spokesmen?"

2. He wondered who the "anonymous" financial sponsors of the ad were.

3. He wondered if the same fifteen would sign another ad, affirming Christian belief in justice in some other country, such as South Africa or the Soviet Union. "Do evangelicals speak out for justice or only for prophecy?" He asked about "the complicated questions of justice involving Israel's dealings with dispossessed Palestinians. Does the assumed fulfillment of prophecy render this question irrelevant?"

4. He called the ad "prophetic maneuvering." Suppose, he said, "that a group of concerned Jews in the year 4 B.C. had placed a full-page ad in the Rome Tribune: 'We the undersigned Jews affirm our belief in Bethlehem as the locale for our Messiah's birth (Micah 5:2). We therefore appeal to Caesar to require an annual census, requiring people in the provinces to return to their hometowns. This action will call back to Bethlehem a dispersed woman who will give birth to the Messiah there.' "

5. He suggested that the Old Testament prophets were "surely aware 'of the promise of the land to the Jewish people. . . .' But they did not hesitate to declare God's judgment on his people, and their consequent

dispossession from the land. I wonder what Jeremiah would have said about such an ad?"

Bayly then asked if the modern Israeli government was "more deserving of God's blessing, and of inheriting the land, than the government under which Jeremiah lived. I think not."

A second recent challenger is Colin Chapman, Regional Secretary (Director) of the International Federation of Evangelical Students for Islamic Lands. In an article for *Crusade* magazine, reprinted in Intervarsity Christian Fellowship's *His*, he found popular books on prophecy "almost entirely lacking" in a "moral dimension. . . . If there is any trace of it at all, it usually amounts to general approval of the establishment of the state of Israel, together with all its policies and actions. These writers seem more concerned to see how events in the Middle East fit into a great historical scheme, than to evaluate the actions of those who are making history. . . . Our preoccupation with the fulfillment of prophecy generally means that we have plenty to say about the Jews, but less to say to the Jews, and even less to say to the Arabs—particularly the Palestinians who feel that the Christian West still hasn't really grasped that the problem of Palestinians is the heart of the whole Middle East problem."

What of the nondispensational view which the great majority of Christian theologians have held through the centuries? As with dispensationalism, we can only present a broad outline.

1. God called Abraham from Mesopotamia to be the father of many nations. The "many nations" refers both to his physical and spiritual descendants. Abraham is "the father of all them that believe . . ." (Romans 4:11), among both Jews and Gentiles.

197

God assured Abraham that he and his descendants would enter and possess the land of Canaan. This earthly promise was fulfilled in the conquest under Joshua.

2. At Sinai God entered into a covenant with the Hebrew descendants of Abraham's grandson Jacob. The covenant prescribed boundaries "from the Red Sea to the sea of the Philistines [the Mediterranean], and from the wilderness [the isthmus of Suez] to the Euphrates," (Exodus 23:31 RSV) which today runs through the middle of present Iraq and Syria.

This covenant was conditioned upon Israel's obedience to Jehovah: "If you obey the commandments of the Lord your God . . . the Lord your God will bless you in the land which you are entering to [possess]. But if your heart turns away, and you will not hear, but are drawn away to worship other gods and serve them, I declare to you this day, that you shall perish; you shall not live long in the land which you are going over the Jordan to enter and possess. . . . And the Lord will scatter you among all the peoples, from one end of the earth to the other" (Deuteronomy 30:15-18; 28:64 RSV). The Israelites, or Jews, were not guaranteed perpetual possession of the land regardless of their behavior, but only if they kept the covenant.

Israel broke the covenant. Pagan kings were brought against them. They were scattered.

3. God covenanted with David for a kingdom. David disappointed God and was not permitted to build the Temple. Solomon, David's son, was allowed to build the Temple but soon desecrated it and broke the covenant. "Since . . . you have not kept my covenant and my statutes which I have commanded you, I will surely tear the kingdom from you and will give it to your servant" (1 Kings 11:11 RSV). This prediction was fulfilled. The

earthly dynasty begun by David ended when Zedekiah was led captive to Babylon (2 Kings 25).

4. God showed His mercy by promising that a remnant would return to the land. This promise was literally fulfilled under Cyrus, Zerubbabel, Ezra, and Nehemiah.

5. God then showed His mercy beyond measure by fulfilling His Old Testament promises to Abraham, Moses, and David through the Messiah, Jesus of Nazareth, who by genealogy was "the son of David, the son of Abraham" (Matthew 1:1 RSV). "He will be great, and will be called the Son of the Most High; and the Lord God will give to him the throne of his father David . . . And of his kingdom there will be no end" (Luke 1:32-33 RSV). In life, death, and resurrection, Jesus was recognized as the Son of David and King of the Jews, though the Jewish leadership rejected him.

His kingdom is everlasting and without borders, while the political kingdom of David was limited in time and space.

6. Old Testament promises concerning the return from exile and restoration of Jerusalem were also linked to the spread of God's grace to all nations, which is implicit in the promise to Abraham that in his seed all the nations are to be blessed. An example is seen in two passages frequently cited by dispensationalists as a description of the millennium rule upon a literal earth: "It shall come to pass in the latter days that the mountain of the house of the Lord shall be established as the highest of the mountains, and shall be raised above the hills; and all the nations shall flow to it, and many peoples shall come, and say: 'Come, let us go up to the mountain of the Lord, to the house of the God of Jacob, that he may teach us his ways and that we may walk in his paths.' For out of Zion shall go forth the law and the word of the Lord from Jerusalem. He shall

judge between the nations, and shall decide for many peoples; and they shall beat their swords into plowshares, and their spears into pruning hooks; nation shall not lift up sword against nation, neither shall they learn war any more" (Isaiah 2:2-4; see also Micah 4:1-3).

7. Such promises should be interpreted in the light of the New Testament and the New Covenant which Christ established. Christ is both priest and sacrifice, Savior and King, fulfiller and fulfillment.

His grace—as poured out on the cross, authenticated in the resurrection, and demonstrated by the Holy Spirit in His people—is available to "whosoever will" receive. Grace is the only grounds for acceptance of sinners by God. This is the principal argument of the book of Romans where Paul shows that both Jews and Gentiles are adjudged sinners before God and become the spiritual children of Abraham only by faith in Christ's saving death.

8. Christ's people from all nations are spiritual Israel. In this Israel, unlike the old, there are no divisions or rankings. They are "Jews" "in the spirit, and not in the letter; whose praise is not of men, but of God" (Romans 2:29). Christ "is our peace, who hath made us both [Jews and Gentiles] one, and hath broken down the middle wall of partition between us; Having abolished in his flesh the enmity . . . for to make in himself of twain one new man, so making peace; And that he might reconcile both unto God in one body by the cross. . . . In whom [Christ] ye are builded together for an habitation of God through the Spirit" (Ephesians 2:14-16, 22). In Christ and true Israel, which is the Church, "There is neither Jew nor Greek . . . bond nor free . . . male nor female: for ye are all one in Christ Jesus" (Galatians 3:28).

9. At the climax of history, the great "Day of the Lord,"

Christ will return. The final great conflict with the forces of evil will then occur. The resurrections and judgments will be accomplished. He will rule over the redeemed of all ages for eternity in the new heavens and new earth.

Great symbolic pictures of these end-time events are presented in Revelation which, in historical context, was written to assure persecuted first-century Christians that Christ will ultimately be victorious over all.

10. Christians of all racial and national groups are called to spread the Good News and to strive for justice among all peoples, realizing in humility that perfect justice can never be achieved until the consummation of the age and the reign of God is effected over all. Justice must flow from the commands of inspired prophets and from power received by the Holy Spirit through personal relationship with God. "He has showed you, O man, what is good; and what does the Lord require of you but to do justice, and to love kindness, and to walk humbly with your God?" (Micah 6:8 RSV).

In striving for justice, we must realize that God is apolitical, transnational, and more concerned about people than structures, affiliations, citizenship, and kinship. He is as concerned about a Palestinian Arab in a refugee camp as a Jew living in Tel Aviv. He loves a member of the Soviet Politburo no less than a United States senator. He is always reaching out in love and mercy to those who choose to receive and obey Him.

Where are these evangelicals who believe that God favors no racial or ethnic group better than another? They are in the Catholic church and the great denominations spawned by the Protestant Reformation: Lutheran, Methodist, Reformed, Presbyterian, and others. They are also in many of the so-called "free" church bodies such as Mennonites and the giant Southern Baptist

Convention. Some of the best known Southern Baptist preachers take the dispensational line, but many others do not. Southern Baptist seminary professors tend overwhelmingly not to accept dispensationalism.

Why is their voice not heard? There are several reasons. One, they have not been as bold and creative in communicating their interpretations of biblical prophecy as have dispensationalists. Two, they have been too mesmerized by ecclesiastical mumbo-jumbo and thought-forms peculiar to their own traditions and organizations. Three, their message is not as marketable as the claims of dispensationalists. Commercial publishers, both secular and religious, know that books on reconciliation and justice do not sell as well as "end-of-the-world" dramas even though they be almost totally void of moral dimension.

There is one other reason for the weakness of the nondispensational voice. Many advocates have feared to speak out boldly, lest they be called anti-Semitic and enemies of Israel. Some have developed close friendships with Jewish rabbis and cannot bring themselves to be critical of Israel for fear of offending.

They do speak in theological journals, commentaries, and in seminary classrooms. They do make valid criticisms of dispensationalism. One is that dispensationalists pick and choose between the literal and the symbolic. Hal Lindsey, for example, takes Scofield's view that Ezekiel 38 refers to Russia and other northern European powers as persecutors of Israel. "The land of Magog" of verse 1, he says, is Russia. "Meshech and Tubal" of that same verse are Moscow and Tobolsk respectively. However, he sees the military equipment (bucklers, shields, helmets, swords, etc.) mentioned in this chapter as symbolic.

In concluding this long chapter, we can only briefly summarize the two general answers from Christendom to the question: Whose side is God on in the Middle East controversy?

Dispensationalists say Israel is the fulfillment of biblical prophecy. Some dispensationalists appear to endorse every Israeli military venture and policy towards Arabs. The more discerning and thoughtful qualify their blessing. The late William Culbertson, long time president of the Moody Bible Institute, said "my heart goes out" to the Arab refugees. This problem, he added, "is the responsibility of Israel, the Arab nations, and the rest of the world." But all dispensationalists say that in the long run of events, God favors Israel.

The nondispensationalists, who identify the Israel of prophecy with the Church, say God sees Israel no differently than He does any of the Arab countries. He is as much on the Jew's side as He is on the Arab's. His concern is with righteousness and justice by all and towards all.

11

The Way to Peace

Theological debates over the future of the Middle East are mainly Western luxuries. Most Arabs and Jews who are directly involved wouldn't know one "dispensation" from another. They want three decades of "tribulation" to end. They want the fighting, bombing, and raiding to stop. They want peace now.

A war-weary Israeli told a *Parade* magazine reporter: "Ever since Sadat's surprise visit here, peace between Israel and her neighbors had become not just a dream, but something you can taste. And nobody wants that taste to go away."

The "taste" has since begun to sour. The once bright hopes have dimmed. Differences between Israel and Egypt and other Arabs seem irreconcilable. Sadat vows "not to give up one inch of Arab ground" in the territories occupied by Israel in 1967. Begin will only go part way.

What are the realistic prospects for a settlement? What is the future of the Palestinians? Is it possible that Israel may be conquered and a secular or Muslim Arab state established in the historic, biblical land? What of the Communist threat? What are Christians, Jews, and Muslims doing constructively for peace? And what more can be done?

Unbelieving cynics, who take the cyclical view of history, say any peace will only be temporary. They believe that history keeps repeating itself, empires rise and fall, wars break out and are resolved, and there are only interludes between hostilities. The world is going nowhere. There is no ultimate purpose or sovereign will. The cycles will continue until man has destroyed his own species, unless he can rise above his habits of the past.

Christians, Muslims, and Jews hold to the linear view of the march of human events. They admit that history often does repeat itself, but in the long run history will climax with the "Day of the Lord."

Dispensational and nondispensational Christians agree that God will end history by His sovereign will and way. They differ on interpretation of biblical details, which include the roles of Israel and the Arabs in the plan of God. This difference greatly influences attitudes on the future of the Middle East.

"Keep your eyes on the Middle East," said Hal Lindsey in *The Late Great Planet Earth*. "If this is the time that we believe it is, this area will become a constant source of tension for all the world. The fear of another World War will be almost completely centered in the troubles of this area. It will become so severe that only Christ or the Antichrist can solve it. Of course the world will choose the Antichrist." No hope for peace here short of the millennium.

Charles Ryrie insists that Israel must expand. He notes that Israel's divine inheritance prescribed in Genesis 15:18 is "from the river of Egypt unto the great river, the river Euphrates. . . ." The "river of Egypt" could be a wady (a stream that is dry part of the year) near Gaza or the Nile. He believes it is the Nile. But he leaves himself an escape valve. Israel, he says, might not regain all this territory until the millennial reign of Christ. "Someday, though," he assures, "the promise will be fulfilled. God always keeps his promise." This prediction is not very comforting to the Arabs.

Dispensational positions have led to time predictions of the return of Christ. Such dating is not new. Thousands of European Christians journeyed to Mount Zion in the year 1000 to await Christ's return there. In 1524 a German astronomer-preacher forecast a flood that would mark the end. His followers built rafts and arks. When the deluge didn't come, they tossed him in a pond.

In 1831 William Miller, a Baptist minister, aroused great excitement in New England by preaching that Bible prophecies pointed to the Second Coming of Christ in 1843. During that year, his followers neglected worldly vocations and gathered on hilltops and in cemeteries to await the great Event. When the year passed, Miller set a new date in 1844. Again his followers disregarded worldly pursuits and gathered to await Christ's return. Miller himself led one band, clad in white ascension gowns, to a Massachusetts hilltop. Once more, he had to revise his dates.

The daters know Christ said "of that day and hour knoweth no man" (Matthew 24:36). They answer much like Moses Berg, the founder of the Children of God cult, "He didn't say we couldn't know the month or year."

Hal Lindsey will not be that specific, but he has

suggested Christ will probably return before 1980.

Some daters have recently been more specific. For example, Dr. Charles Taylor, a respected California dispensationalist, had thousands believing Christ would "rapture" His Church in September 1976. Taylor based his "real possibility" on an interpretation of Matthew 24:34: "Verily I say unto you, This generation shall not pass, till all these things be fulfilled." Taylor pegged the generation designated as starting the year modern Israel became a state. He arrived at the length of a generation from Job 42:16 where Job was said to have lived "an hundred and forty years . . . even four generations" after his deliverance. Four divided into 140 equals 35 years for one generation. Then he added 35 to 1948 and got 1983 which he decided was the year Christ would return in power and glory at the end of the seven-year Tribulation. Nineteen-eighty-three minus seven gave him 1976 for the Rapture. Taylor has since pushed the time further ahead.

Dating will continue until the time Christ actually returns. He has already delayed His coming over nineteen hundred years. He could wait another century or millennium. Many Christians quote Matthew 24:14 in saying His return is not immediate: "And this gospel of the kingdom shall be preached in all the world for a witness unto all nations; and then shall the end come." Some missionary analysts say half the world's population has yet to hear about Jesus the Messiah.

Bill Bright, head of Campus Crusade for Christ, does "not personally believe that the Lord's return is imminent. I think the current teaching that it is imminent is leading many, many Christians to fold their hands and disobey what Jesus said to do," he said in *Christianity Today*. "Jesus said we should work, for the night is coming when no man can work. According to Scripture, he has delayed his return in order that more people might have a chance to hear."

Paul Rees, vice-president of World Vision (noted for Christian relief ministries), wrote in *World Vision Magazine:* "I shall go to my grave believing that, side by side with my ardent expectation of the Second Advent, most of our 'signs of the times' sermons and books are based on opportunism and a mistaken understanding of what the apocalyptic portions of Scripture are meant to teach us. These hot sermonic and literary outpourings tend, in the case of many Christians, to distract from the 'occupy until I come' mandate for missions and social responsibility."

Catholic charismatic leader Gabriel Meyer of Los Angeles is likewise negative. Lindsey's books, Meyer told the *Los Angeles Times*, are "a problem" to the Catholic charismatic movement. "We don't encourage it [talk of the Rapture and a precise timetable] because it can produce an other-worldly, I'm-on-the-winning-team attitude."

The various evangelical missions to the Jews hold a slightly different perspective on a Mideast solution. Though dispensational, they major on evangelization of Jews. Some believe that the return will be preceded by a massive turning to Christ among Jews.

A remarkable number of young American Jews have become "Messianic" or "completed" Jews, the terms used to describe Jews who have accepted Christ as the fulfillment of the Torah, the priestly sacrifice system, and Old Testament messianic prophecies. Estimates range from 3,000 upwards to 100,000. Disturbed Jewish leaders complain of "false witnessing." Members of the extremist Jewish Defense League have allegedly attacked some of the "Jews for Jesus" evangelists. Jewish opponents say that a Jew can't accept Jesus and continue as a Jew. Moishe Rosen, leader of "Jews for Jesus," counters that Messianic Jews are more Jewish than ever.

Rosen readily admits that present Israel is no messianic state. Messianic Jews in Israel are said to number no more than three hundred, and some of these were won to Christ outside Israel. Rosen concedes that injustices may have been committed against the Palestinians. He believes that God's special prophetic purposes do not absolve Israel from any wrongs inflicted on Arabs.

Nor do respected evangelical magazines excuse Israel from judgment. Said *Christianity Today*, during the initial Sadat-Begin negotiations: "Because some Christians believe that the restoration of the State of Israel is a fulfillment of biblical prophecy, they think that opposing the Israeli government is the same as opposing God. Such an attitude is only possible for those who do not understand the difference between what God has revealed to us as our responsibilities and what God has told us will happen. . . . Christians should form their political, ethical, and military judgments on the basis of general principles for nations and for justice that are revealed in Scripture."

Christianity Today still believes "there is a strong case for the right of Israel to exist securely and peacefully. This case can be made by appealing to biblical as well as to commonly accepted standards. Christians everywhere should promote peace in the Middle East. And that surely means that some provision must be made for the displaced Palestinians. Until they have been settled, there can be no peace."

Christianity Today has always leaned to the dispensational view of prophecy. In the editorial just cited, the editors come close to the position of nondispensationalists who say that the establishment of Israel in 1948 was an injustice to the Palestinians, but that Israel has the right to exist.

The nondispensationalists base this right not upon ancestral or religious rights, but upon the fact that Israel now exists as a state and that the Arabs can do nothing about it. The Arabs respond that before 1948 Israel as a state did not exist and the population of the area was then largely Arab. The formation of the state of Israel changed the status quo and Arabs have the right to make similar political alterations.

Anwar Sadat was the first Arab leader to recognize Israel as a sovereign state. "I never thought I'd see that in my lifetime," says Dr. Sholomo Avineri, noted Israeli political analyst and a leader in the Israeli Labor Party. "Sadat accepting the legitimacy of Israel."

Avineri's party is the loyal opposition to Begin's hard-line Likud. Both major parties agree that Israel's existence as a nation cannot be traded away. Both concur that there can never be a real Mideast peace until other Arab countries recognize the sovereignty of Israel, as Egypt has done.

Beyond this, there are major foreign policy differences between them. Says Avineri, who served as director-general of Israel's Ministry of Foreign Affairs when Labor was in power, "The position of Mr. Begin's Likud Party is simply to wage wars and end opposition . . . while we are willing to seriously negotiate for peace."

Avineri places the basic conflict in the Middle East between Arab nationalism and Jewish nationalism. The "religious issue," he says, "is only one factor in Jewish nationalism, as is the persecution issue.

"The question is not wrong against right from either point of view. It is one of right against right. The Arabs

are right and Israel is right. We clash over the same piece
of land, and each of us feels this is ours, exclusively ours.

"In this situation neither of us can have all his rights.
Each must give."

The "give" must come in the territories occupied by
Israel in 1967. Giving back the Sinai to Egypt and the
Golan Heights to Syria is not a big problem, "so long as
provision is made for Israel's security," Avineri says.
"These lands are not part of our heritage. The difficulty
comes over the West Bank and Gaza. The Labor Party
recognizes that this is our land and our heritage. The
question is, do we maintain it or do we trade it in for
peace?"

Avineri recognizes that the Palestinians in Gaza and
the West Bank do not want to live under Israeli rule.
"We [the Labor Party] are not interested in maintaining
control and rule over Palestinians who don't want us. But
we can't accept a PLO state on the West Bank. The PLO is
out to destroy us. Perhaps a union or federation of the
West Bank with Jordan."

The PLO says it wants to replace Israel with a
Palestinian state in which the three religions—Judaism,
Christianity, and Islam—would have equal
representation. "We've always made a distinction
between Judaism and Zionism," insists Yasser Arafat.

The PLO is willing to accept a Palestinian state in the
West Bank and Gaza for the present. Not even the Israeli
moderates will consent to a PLO state so close to Israel.

The Arab countries want a Palestinian state but not
necessarily under the PLO. They prefer a more moderate
and predictable Palestinian government, though for
diplomatic and security reasons few Arab politicians will
say so.

If the PLO could be nudged out of the picture
(something that is hardly likely), the question of who will

control Jerusalem will remain.

Old Jerusalem, which includes the Muslim holy places, is part of the West Bank area taken in 1967. Begin says he will not negotiate on this. Sadat says "no Muslim will agree to let the Arab sector[part of old Jerusalem] remain under the sovereignty of Israel." Sadat will accept internationalization, but only if "it includes the entire city, not just the Arab part."

One possible compromise is suggested by Dr. Sana Hassan, an Egyptian political scholar. She thinks Jerusalem's defense "might be entrusted" to the Israeli army, with the city jointly administered by Jews and Arabs, and the holy places of Judaism, Christianity, and Islam given a neutral status.

To sum up: The prospects for settlement now center on the status of occupied territories, which includes old Jerusalem. It is a matter of bending on both sides. Sadat has made the first bow, while Begin has hardly tipped his hat. Begin must make a dramatic shift to keep the peace talks going. If he does, he could be in trouble with the hawks of his own party. If he does not, the fragile rapport built up between the Egyptians and Israelis may soon break down. Or a more moderate government could come to power in Israel which would reach an agreement with first Egypt, and then the Palestinians and other Arab nations.

Should the impasse continue, there is the grave possibility of another war. And if there is a settlement, tensions are likely to continue.

The Soviet Union, which has long tried to exploit Middle East troubles, does not want a war. Neither does the Communist superpower want a solid peace. *Christianity Today* diagnosed Soviet designs perfectly: The "leaders want the situation to simmer so that they can regain some of the influence that they have lost in the past few years. The Soviets want a Palestinian state that would be dependent on them to emerge on part of the territory not controlled by Israel."

The Soviets supported Israel in the beginning, perhaps in hopes of driving a wedge between the West and the Arabs. The Soviets did not fully support the Arabs until 1956.

Arab leaders have long memories and are wary of Soviet duplicity. They know that the Soviets define "truth" and "right" in terms of their own best interests. They are aware of what happened in Egypt.

The Soviets were ensconced in Egypt until 1972 when Sadat ordered fifteen thousand of their military experts home. "The Soviets wanted Egypt to be their agents," Sadat told CBS-TV's Mike Wallace. Sadat further wrote in his biography (*In Search of Identity*, Harper & Row, 1978): "The Soviets had thought at one time that they had Egypt in their pocket, and the world had come to think that the Soviet Union was our guardian. I wanted to tell the Russians that the will of Egypt was entirely Egyptian."

During their stay in Egypt, the Russians stirred plots all over the Arab world. They scored their biggest success in Iraq in 1958 when Iraqi Communists killed young King Feisal II. The new Iraqi leaders then conspired with Russian and Egyptian Communists to overthrow Feisal's Jordanian cousin, King Hussein. For a time Jordan was encircled and cut off from oil supplies, while Communist agents inside the country organized assassin squads. An American airlift helped ease the oil problem. And by a miracle of sorts, Hussein escaped assassination and saved the country.

Hussein's feelings about Communism during this

critical time are spelled out in his biography, *Uneasy Lies The Head* (Bernard Geis Associates, 1962): "I stood firmly behind my belief that Communism could never help the liberation of the Arab peoples . . . because the ultimate end of Communism must be a form of slavery and obedience to Moscow. Communism could never be an ally of nationalism because nationalism is a major threat to Communism."

More recently the Soviets have been making a comeback by supplying arms to the PLO, Iraq (which now has a non-Communist government), Syria, Algeria, and the little Marxist state of South Yemen. Some of the arms payments come by way of Saudi Arabia, which also gives aid to the Egyptian economy. But this doesn't mean the Saudis are entranced with Communism.

The Saudi rulers are implacable foes of Communism. Their kingdom is a monarchy and they fear a Communist-style revolution. And as the most devout Muslims in the Middle East, they will have no truck with atheism.

The late King Feisal of Saudi Arabia, who was assassinated by a demented nephew in 1975, equated Communism with Zionism. He was angriest over Jewish control of the Muslim holy places in Jerusalem, and his lifelong dream was to pray in the Mosque of Omar before he died. He never did.

Arab political analysts believe Communism can only win among the Arabs if the U.S. maintains a one-sided policy of backing Israel. They say Arab leaders are encouraged by Jimmy Carter's tough stance against Begin's refusal to return all occupied territories and his talk of a Palestinian homeland.

Recent interviews in Lebanon, Jordan, and Egypt reveal enormous admiration by Muslims for Jimmy

Carter, the Christian. A Jordanian businessman expressed a common assessment of Carter: "Your President Carter is not only a Christian; he is also a true believer. There is a difference, you know."

Arab leaders have long been frustrated that most Western Christians do not understand Arab aspirations. Sadat and Hussein are encouraging tourism from the West to biblical and other historic sites in their countries. Their economies also badly need more foreign exchange. During the initial stage of the negotiations with Israel, Sadat mentioned wanting to build an interfaith chapel on Mount Sinai, if and when the Sinai region is returned by Israel, where Muslims, Jews, and Christians can join in prayer. Later, on July 31, 1978, Sadat was quoted in a slightly different vein by an Associated Press dispatch from Alexandria, Egypt. The Egyptian president told the AP reporter that he wanted to build a Jewish temple, a Muslim mosque, and a Christian church on Mount Sinai, as a peace symbol.

Sadat has been rolling out the carpet to prominent American Christians and Jews. One of the first visitors after Sadat's historic flight to Jerusalem was the Reverend Harald Bredesen of Escondido, California. Bredesen went in February, 1978, to film an interview with Sadat for airing on the Christian Broadcasting Network's "700 Club." Received warmly, Bredesen asked Sadat to join with other Arab leaders and Israel's Begin in calling Muslims, Jews, and Christians to observe a "day of prayer for peace in the Middle East." Bredesen hopes that President Carter will issue a similar proclamation.

Said Bredesen, "Ever since Israel's rebirth, we evangelicals have had our arm around her. I'm not suggesting we take it away, but that we put our other around Egypt, that we reach out in love to Sadat and the

Egyptian people just as we have to Israel. Maybe evangelical Christians have a role to play in bringing Jews and Arabs together."

Near the time of Bredesen's visit, Sadat entertained a team of American rabbis. After an hour's talk, the president of the Jewish Theological Seminary remarked, "Sadat is doing for Jews and Muslims what Pope John did for Catholics and Protestants."

Sadat emphasizes that Jews and Christians have complete freedom of religion in Egypt, and that Jews are not leaving any more. Sadat is proud that the law recently proposed by Egyptian Muslim extremists making conversion from Islam a capital crime was killed, while Israel was voting in a conversion law punishable by imprisonment if "material inducement" to convert could be proved.

Sadat would also like Western Christians to see that Christianity is flourishing in Egypt more than in Israel. He points with pride to the large established Coptic church, the Coptic Evangelical church, and a number of smaller groups. "Christians fought alongside Muslims in our wars against Israel," he says.

The Coptic Evangelical church, with thirty thousand members, is the largest Protestant denomination in the Middle East. It was started by United Presbyterian missionaries in 1854. It now has its own missionary and social service agencies.

The Coptic Evangelical Organization for Social Services (CEOSS) is outstanding. CEOSS serves thousands of poor villages along the Nile. (Per capita annual income in Egypt is only $345; villagers earn only an average of $60.) Ministries include adult literacy and education, agriculture, homemaking, health care, family life service, handcrafts, publishing and leadership training. CEOSS is the only non-Muslim agency in Egypt licensed to import and export books. A recent title is *The Life and Teachings of Jesus the Messiah*, written especially for Muslims, and distributed as a cooperative project between CEOSS, Baptist Publications of Lebanon, and the David C. Cook Foundation of Illinois.

CEOSS director, Dr. Samuel Habib, received his theological training in the U.S. He has a staff of 106 "supervisors" who live in villages and supervise local volunteers. "We serve the whole village," Habib declares. "Christians and Muslims, we tell them all that our work is an expression of God's love and is for everybody. The people see a new life in our staff and the volunteers. Many respond to the gospel."

Seventy-five per cent of CEOSS's support comes from the Arab world. United Presbyterian women in the U.S. are among the biggest supporters abroad. "We could train many more leaders if we had more aid," Habib says.

The Assemblies of God and Free Methodists also have strong church bodies in Egypt. The Assemblies have 144 churches and 12,100 recognized believers. Their most notable ministry is the American orphanage at Assiut. It was opened in 1923 by the late Lillian Thrasher, who was perhaps the best loved foreign woman in Egypt in this century. The orphanage has cared for over seven thousand orphans and widows. Many Egyptian Assembly pastors were first introduced to Christ by "The Nile Mother," as Miss Thrasher was affectionately known.

The emphasis among all evangelical groups in Egypt is on national leadership. The director of Campus Crusade for Christ, for example, is Mouri Faraghallah, the son of a beloved evangelical pastor. Faraghallah was a banker for twenty-nine years before becoming a full-time staff member of the world-wide evangelistic organization. He is also a playwright and holds master's degrees in both literature and banking. One of his brothers is an admiral in the Egyptian navy, another a medical doctor, another an accountant. A sister is headmistress at a leading school in Alexandria. "All are Christians," Faraghallah says with delight. "Each has some kind of ministry in a church.

"There is now more freedom to proclaim the gospel in Egypt than I can ever remember," he says. "We already have work on five campuses in major cities. There are a half-million college students in Egypt. We train Christian students to win others and to disciple them."

Also in Egypt, a vigorous spiritual awakening is occurring in some parts of the old Coptic church. But the leader of the renewal, Father Zacharia Botros, has reportedly been reprimanded by his superior for his religious beliefs.

Father Zacharia, as he is known throughout Egypt, preaches that through Bible study he came into a deep spiritual relationship with Christ a few years ago and as a result has experienced the power of the Holy Spirit. He claims that a number of persons have been healed physically and emotionally in his meetings. He admits also having spoken privately in tongues, but does not promote this "gift" in services.

What alarmed his superiors was his teaching that the established Coptic church has raised good works and church tradition to the same level as grace and faith in the doctrine of salvation. Pope Shenouda III, the leader of the Copts, once suspended the so-called charismatic priest from his pulpit. However, he did not take away Zacharia's church standing. The priest began leading Bible studies and preaching in Copt churches throughout Egypt. One Bible study, at the famous St. Mark's Cathedral in Cairo, has attracted upwards of three thousand people.

Hundreds have reportedly been converted and baptized under Zacharia's ministry, including an estimated two hundred former Muslims. There are fears that Zacharia's popularity and success may incite opposition from radical Muslims in Egypt.

Jordan has a much smaller Christian population than Egypt. Over half the forty resident Western missionaries are affiliated with two Baptist agencies, the Southern Baptist Convention, and the Conservative Baptist Foreign Mission Society. Their work is highly respected.

King Hussein's three young children attend the Southern Baptist day school in Amman. How this happened is an interesting story.

In 1970 the Southern Baptist mission purchased five acres of land for $100,000. (The land is now worth a million dollars!) They put another $150,000 on a building and announced the school opening in 1974. They planned for an enrollment of seventy-five children, but after a week of "registration" only four children had been signed up. "We were so discouraged," recalls Paul Smith, the present chairman of the mission. "I was walking around the empty playground saying, 'Lord, why did you lead us up this blind alley?' My wife, Virginia, and the other teachers were up in the school praying for more children. About that time a little red Mercedes convertible, followed by two security cars, rolled up. It was the wife of the Crown Prince. She asked us some questions, then asked if we'd accept her daughter. Then the queen came and we enrolled her children. After that we had no trouble making our enrollment."

Smith, whom the king calls "a very dear friend," says Hussein has taken a deep personal interest in the school. "One morning his Highness stopped to visit. I took him to chapel. He heard the Bible stories and the prayers, then listened to the children sing the Jordanian National Anthem. When they finished with 'long live the King,' I looked back and tears were rolling down his cheeks."

The fastest growing Baptist church is in Zarka, the second largest city in Jordan. "They have some Pentecostal tendencies," Smith says. "They raise their hands when they pray and occasionally someone speaks in tongues. I myself don't, but I recognize their sincerity. We missionaries discussed their worship and some wondered if we shouldn't interfere. I said, 'Let them develop as they wish.' Southern Baptists have traditionally not been with the Pentecostals. When they have a revival, we don't. I feel very strongly that we're the losers for that. But some in the mission don't share my feelings. That's all right. We're a democratic group."

The center of Christian missionary work in the Middle East has long been in Lebanon. Before the tragic 1976 civil war, twenty-seven separate Protestant missions reported 195 workers. Most were in Beirut which was then the commercial center and the gateway to the Arab world.

The best known missionary landmark in embattled Lebanon is the American University. Founded by Presbyterians, this school has educated more Arab leaders than any other similar institution. In recent decades it has become more secularized.

Alumni include the two most noted radical Palestinian *fedayeen*, Drs. Wadi Haddad and George Habash. Haddad who died in 1978 from an "incurable disease," was a pediatrician and the reported mastermind behind some of the most shocking terrorist actions of the 1970s. Habash, who has a Christian background, leads the Popular Front for the Liberation of Palestine which acts independently of the PLO.

Lebanese Presbyterian churches have declined in recent years. A number of sanctuaries are only empty hulks. Some evangelical missionaries say the decline was caused by liberal theology among missionary teachers. By contrast, United Presbyterian representatives in Egypt are reported to be more Bible-centered than their colleagues in Lebanon.

What unites most missionaries in Lebanon, conservatives and liberals, is empathy for the Palestinian cause. After the Six-Day War, sixty-six representatives of twelve American agencies signed a letter of concern, urging their constituents:

(1) To put away "stereotypes" of Arabs. "Too many Westerners assume that all [Palestinian] Arabs are nomadic tribesmen, whereas the great proportion of homeless refugees from Palestine have been farmers, villagers, and city-dwellers. . . . The slogan, 'But see how the Israelis have made the desert bloom' is misleading, and even if . . . true, better agricultural performance does not confer property rights."

(2) "To try to dig out the facts, both of the present situation and of the historical events that led up to [the Arab-Israeli conflict]. For example, the Israelis insist that the refugees both of 1948 and of 1967 left their homes of their own free will, misled by their Arab leadership. We who live here, however, know that there has always been a great deal of pressure, and not a little force, to 'encourage' the Arabs to leave."

(3) "To try to understand the feelings on both sides. . . . Westerners in general are already aware of what the Israeli feels: pride that he is once more, after so long, master in Palestine, where he no longer need apologize for being Jewish. But Westerners are not so aware of what the Arab feels: resentment at losing his land, humiliation

at military losses, frustration at being unable to make his claims understood to the rest of the world."

(4) "To challenge the assumption that might makes right. . . . Whatever Israel intends to do with the land [taken in 1967], many Christians will assume she has the right to do it. Isn't it too simple to assume that all this military action is a manifestation of God's grace?"

(5) "To challenge the assumption that the Israeli occupation . . . of large portions of Palestine, represents the fulfillment of prophecy. . . . If Jesus made it clear that God is to be worshiped neither on Mt. Gerizim nor in Jerusalem (John 4:21), can Christians believe that God's promise is fulfilled by the occupation of Palestine by the modern political state of Israel?"

(6) To recognize that "the Christian obligation is to minister to the last, the least, and the lost of this world. Just as Christians were called upon to . . . relieve the suffering of Jewish victims of Nazi persecution, so now we are called upon to do all within our power to relieve the suffering Arab refugees."

(7) "To seek not only to bind up wounds but to prevent new ones: and this means working not only through our own church agencies but also through our government and the United Nations. The state of Israel should therefore be held to the UN resolution of November 22, 1967, calling for a withdrawal of Israeli troops from the areas occupied after June 5, 1967. . . ."

"We urge you," they concluded, "to look beyond the one-sided reporting and opinions current in the West, to be sensitive and responsible to the present Middle Eastern tragedy, and to pray and work for a reconciliation which is based on real justice."

In April 1974 many of these same missionaries participated in a thirty-mile Palestinian Peace March in

Lebanon organized by the American Peace March Committee. At the end of the march, Southern Baptist missionary Jess Willmon addressed a crowd of fifteen thousand Arab Muslims in Tyre, probably the largest Muslim audience ever to hear a Christian missionary in person.

James Newton, editor of the Southern Baptist *World Mission Journal* interviewed his denomination's missionaries afterwards and found that most missionaries had rejected the "theory . . . that events in the Middle East are fulfillment of biblical prophecies. . . . Yet they are quick to say they are not 'anti-Semitic.' "

Wayne Fuller told Newton that he and his wife, Frances, were working in Jordan when the 1967 war came. ". . . We started seeing the refugees fleeing. Almost everyone had run from Israel until they could run no more. They walked as fast as they could. One woman really touched me. Her legs were swollen beyond recognition and her feet were bleeding. Yet she still carried her child in her arms all of the way. The child was clutched so tightly that it hurt her just to sit down. Her face was creased with anguish. My attitude drastically changed after that incident."

Frances Fuller, who directs Baptist Publications in Beirut, spoke of a "very dear Palestinian friend. Recently she went back to visit relatives in Israel. She still had the deed to her land. Tears came to her eyes, but she still had the strength to knock at the door of her home. The family living in the house allowed her to come in. There she saw them sitting on the chairs and sofa that her money had bought and she saw that they were sleeping on her beds. When she excused herself sadness was in her heart. She was leaving her own home."

Executives of the Southern Baptist Foreign Mission

Board asked Newton not to print the "political" opinions of Baptist missionaries in Lebanon. (The *World Missions Journal* is published by a separate Southern Baptist agency.) But he went ahead and added an editorial calling for Israeli withdrawal of lands occupied in 1967. He did include a statement of "official" Board policy that said in part: ". . . The sympathies of missionaries usually lie with the people among whom they work. The Foreign Mission Board respects their freedom of thought and action, but asks that they not use it in such a way as to endanger their missionary colleagues or their fellow Christians or to jeopardize the witness for Christ anywhere. . . . Missionaries who are quoted in this article are not speaking for the Foreign Mission Board or their colleagues in the Middle East."

This is generally the position of other Western mission agencies in the Middle East. But many missionaries are not happy. "You have put my conscience in a terrible bind," Frances Fuller told a Southern Baptist Board official.

There are around one hundred registered Christian missionaries in Israel. About half of these are Southern Baptists who carry on cultural, educational, and agricultural ministries with both Arabs and Jews. These missionaries have kept their political beliefs largely to themselves for obvious reasons. The free-lance missionaries who come in and out of the country on tourist visas are not so reticent about defending Israeli policies.

Southern Baptists also operate hospitals in Jordan, Gaza, and North Yemen. The workers in Yemen are forbidden by the Muslim government to hold public services or to directly evangelize patients. The only missionary casualty of the Middle East conflict was nurse Mavis Pate in Gaza. On the evening of January 16, 1972, she and other missionaries were traveling from Gaza to Tel Aviv when their Volkswagen Microbus was ambushed by Palestinians near a refuge camp. Missionary Ed Nicholas and one of his three daughters were wounded in the attack that killed Miss Pate. The missionary surgeon, Dr. Merrill D. Moore, called the ambush a case of mistaken identity.

Still another highly respected Western Christian agency in the Middle East is the Mennonite Central Committee which has had self-help social ministries in Egypt, Jordan, and Israel since 1950. The MCC calls itself "A Christian Resource for Meeting Human Need" and operates much like CEOSS in Egypt. "You give a man a shirt today and in six months he needs another," says John Hubert, the recent MCC director in Jordan. "Help him improve his farm or begin a business and he can buy his own shirt."

MCC's young staffers are pacifists and strongly opposed to violence. But they identify strongly with the Palestinians. "We care when people are exploited," Paul Quiring, director of West Bank operations, told two U.S. congressional staff committees studying Middle East problems. Quiring testified that "the majority" of Israeli settlements on the West Bank "have been built on land which was not sold but was either expropriated or confiscated." In the village of Akraba, he said, twelve hundred acres of village farmland had been fenced off for "security reasons."

Quiring and other MCC staff members insist they support Israel's right to exist, but "the Palestinians must have the right to self-determination and statehood as well."

The Mennonites do little evangelizing. Most other Christian agencies evangelize vigorously, principally through radio broadcasts, literature distribution, correspondence courses, and tape cassettes.

The usual procedure for getting correspondence students is to run newspaper ads and make radio solicitations for free courses by mail. Christianity is not mentioned in the ads. Students are then followed up with personal visits and/or cassette Bible studies.

One mission sends cassettes to "home fellowships" in thirteen Arab countries. Most of the "believers" are Muslims who have accepted Jesus as their Messiah and Savior. Another wrote 120 of its students in a North African Arab country, saying, "We would like to visit and teach you more about Christ." Eighty-six responded with an invitation.

North African Arab countries are closed to "professional" missionaries. Workers go in as doctors, nurses, engineers, English teachers, etc., and share their faith in private encounters. The North Africa Mission has 102 of these "tentmakers" and believes Muslims are more open to the gospel than "nominal, unsaved Christians" in the historic churches.

The reputable evangelical Christian missions make no apologies for witnessing to Muslims and also Jews. On Islam, some quote Kenneth Cragg, one of the foremost Christian authorities on Muslim-Christian relations. "If Christ is what Christ is, he must be uttered. If Islam is what Islam is, that 'must' is irresistible. Wherever there is misconception, witness must penetrate; wherever there is obscuring of the beauty of the cross, it must be unveiled; wherever men have missed God in Christ, he must be brought to them again. . . . We present Christ for the sole sufficient reason that he deserves to be presented."

North American Christian leaders have planned a

pace-setting consultation on Muslim evangelization in Colorado Springs in October 1978. The conference coordinator, Donald McCurry, calls for a bold and more understanding witness to Muslims. "We're taking a hard, new look at the problem of culture change. We're finding that 95 per cent of what we Christians do is because of our culture, and not Christianity. The way we dress. The positions in which we pray. The buildings in which we worship. The organization of our worship. Things like that. In the past we've tried to force Muslim believers into Western cultural molds and it hasn't worked very well.

"One concept we're considering," continues McCurry, "is the 'Messianic Mosque.' If Jewish believers in Jesus can have 'Messianic synagogues,' why can't Muslim believers have a worship in harmony with their forms? It seems to me that the problem of Muslims accepting Jesus is mainly the cultural, linguistic, and ethnic barriers that exist between us."

McCurry and Christians of like mind believe that the real solution to conflict in the Middle East and everywhere else is reconciliation and brotherhood in Christ. Jews and Arabs, they say, can find a mutual love for one another through Christ that transcends and overcomes the accumulated enmities of the past.

Some heartwarming examples have occurred. Take an incident at a conference of Miami pastors where the venerable Jewish Christian evangelist Hyman Appleman called Anis Shorrosh, the Palestinian evangelist, to the platform.

Appleman put an arm around the Palestinian and said, "Brethren, herein is the power of God demonstrated. Only in Christ can Arab and Jew be united."

Then in the tradition of the Middle East, he kissed the younger preacher. The Arab returned the kiss. The emotional scene brought tears to the preachers.

Arabs and Jews united in Jesus.

Arabs loving Jews because of Jesus.

Jews loving Arabs because of Jesus.

This can happen, too.

In November 1973 Anis Shorrosh took a choir from the First Baptist Church of Merritt Island, Florida, to perform in Israel. They sang in a hospital to Israeli soldiers, wounded in the recently concluded war. Said the Palestinian, whose father was killed by Jewish soldiers, "I love you because of Jesus."

The taste for peace in the Middle East must not be allowed to go away. There is much that Christians, Muslims, and Jews can do beyond missionary work. We can try to better understand one another's religious and political feelings. We can maintain our personal beliefs while listening to those of other faiths. At a dialogue in staunchly Muslim Libya, attended by the ruler of that country, foreign Catholic priests and Muslim scholars embraced one another in tears.

We in the West can work to change the impression in the Middle East that Christianity is anti-Arab. The anti-Arab image which Christianity bears has resulted in such intense Muslim pressure upon Christians in some areas that many Arab Christian leaders have emigrated abroad. The Christian and Missionary Alliance's Norman Camp in Jordan ruefully said, "Moving to Chicago and Detroit has become a disease."

We can further ask our elected representatives in government to strive for a fair political peace, through the UN and through other diplomacy, that guarantees security to both Jews and Arabs in the Middle East.

All Christians, Jews, and Muslims can rejoice when that peace comes. All will have better opportunities to share their faiths. Christians can show their fellow monotheists, who also believe in the God of Abraham, that true Christianity is love, not persecution; giving, not taking.

And the end-time events of the future? We can agree to disagree and leave the fulfillment of divine purposes to the Sovereign Lord of history.

Shalom! Salaam! Peace!

God help us all.

Sources

We have long wanted to write a book on Arabs, Christians, and Jews in the Middle East that presents both sides. Publisher after publisher declined because of the explosive and divisive opinions which exist among American Christians and because of the strong feelings among so many American evangelicals that there is only one right side. One publisher told us frankly, "We published one book that some thought was favorable to the Arabs. It hurt our image in the evangelical market. We'll never publish another." A close editor friend for a magazine advised, "If you know what's good for you, you'll stay out of this can of worms. Some Christian bookstores may refuse to sell any of your books." This was sobering since our income is earned from free-lance book writing.

Finally we wrote Dan Malachuk, publisher of Logos

International and he immediately said, "Let's do it. It's time for such a book." Dan added that he had long had a personal interest in the Middle East and that Logos has sponsored seminars annually for Arab pastors since 1975; Logos has planned an Arab Christian Leadership Conference for late 1978 in Jordan.

Some will ask: Are two free-lance writers qualified to write authoritatively on such a difficult subject? We first reply that this is basically a reporting documentary. It is not so essential that readers know our opinions, as that they understand the facts and feelings on all sides: the sides of Israel and the Arabs and the sides of prophetic dispensationalists and nondispensationalists among Western evangelicals.

But reporters should be qualified by experience and research. We cite the following:

We were both schooled in the dispensational view of prophecy. We have heard scores of prophecy sermons, read dozens of prophecy books, and used the *Scofield Reference Bible* for many years. Like so many other evangelicals, our first exposure to the Middle East was through dispensational teaching. We simply took it for granted that the establishment of Israel in 1948 was fulfillment of prophecy.

We have written one book about the history of the Jews (now out of print) and another about the experiences of young Messianic Jews in America.* We have spent many hours conversing with "completed" Jews who fervently believe that Israel has a special place with God. We love these and other Jewish friends dearly.

During the past decade we have done on-the-scene research and written other books about Christian ministries in the shadow of war, in the Dominican Republic, Vietnam, Bangladesh, and the Middle East.

---

* *The New Jews*, Tyndale House Publishers, Wheaton, Ill. 1971.

We have been under hostile fire with missionaries. We have seen missionaries tenderly bathing and scraping the feet of disfigured lepers. We have looked helplessly at tiny babies lying on the ground while their starving mothers hovered over them with shrunken breasts and a sad-eyed Muslim doctor remarked, "These babies will die within a week if they do not get some nourishment." Between these trips we have watched affluent, healthy American Christians perusing their prophecy books and running to and fro to hear the latest pulpit pronouncement on "the next event in God's timetable for the Middle East." These observations drove us to consider in greater depth what the Bible says about Christian compassion and ministry to the less fortunate.

Our burden to do a book on the Middle East began during a trip to Lebanon in 1968, a year after the Six-Day War. A trip through southern Lebanon and a visit with an Arab pastor were unforgettable. Said the missionary, "The pastor risked his life by inviting us into his house." Why? "Because we are American Christians, and the Muslims here believe that we are allied with their Zionist enemies. Anyone accused of helping Zionists is in danger." Later, in Beirut, missionaries and Arab church leaders provided a briefing on the Arab side of the conflict. One veteran pastor observed, "Every time an American preacher is quoted in the press as saying that the state of Israel is the fulfillment of prophecy, we get the repercussions here."

There have been two more trips to the Middle East. Marti visited Palestinian refugee camps, Jerusalem and other biblical cities in Israel, and talked with missionaries, Jews, and Arabs (both Christians and Muslims) in Cairo, Amman, and Beirut.

Beyond this, we have read and indexed dozens of

histories, documentaries, and other books from both the Arab and Israeli points of view, as well as commentaries and theological studies of biblical eschatology by both dispensational and nondispensational scholars. Additionally, we have studied news reports from the Middle East, dating from 1948 to the present, and have read every political and religious analysis we could find.

Our single-spaced index of our sources, including many hours of personal interviews in the Middle East, came to over one hundred pages.

Some readers will be disappointed that we have not provided a bibliography of all our sources. The time frame for completion of the book made this impossible. We suggest that interested readers wishing political views from both Arab and Jewish perspectives visit their local library. For those wanting to study the dispensational interpretation of Bible prophecy, we suggest books by members of the faculty of Dallas Theological Seminary, particularly Dr. Charles C. Ryrie, who is dean of that seminary's graduate school and a greatly respected scholar. For the nondispensational view, we recommend George E. Ladd's *Commentary on the Revelation* (Eerdmans Publishing Company, 1971) and *Worthy Is The Lamb* by Ray Summers (Broadman Press, 1951). Dr. Summers is the former chairman of the Religion Department of Baylor University. Dr. Ladd is professor of New Testament Exegesis and Theology at Fuller Theological Seminary.

Hal Lindsey's popular best sellers are available in almost every bookstore and in many drugstores. A critical study of Lindsey's *The Late Great Planet Earth* is titled *Is This Really the End?* and authored by George C. Miladin (Mack Publishing Company, 1972). Another critique of Lindsay's end-times theology is in the Summer 1975 issue of Southern Baptist Theological Seminary's *Review and Expositor*. This issue was devoted entirely to eschatology and the revival of apocalyptic literature. Some back copies may still be purchased from the seminary at 2825 Lexington Road, Louisville, Kentucky 40206.

Excellent bibliographies of additional source books can be obtained from The Zionist Organization of America (4 E. 34th Street, New York, New York 10016) and the Arab Information Center (747 Third Avenue, New York, New York 10017). The embassies of Middle Eastern countries also have material available for researchers.

Two more excellent sources are: (1) Americans for Middle East Understanding, Inc. (Room 538, 475 Riverside Drive, New York, New York 10027) which publishes *The Link*, a magazine dealing with religious and moral issues in the Middle East conflict. The nondispensational, amillennial view of biblical eschatology is generally espoused and articles are written by both liberal and conservative Christian scholars. (2) *Events*, the most informative secular news magazine of the Middle East. Published in Beirut, it is available by subscription from 67/71 Southhampton Row, London WC1 B4ET.

Finally, we suggest reading the Bible, both Old and New Testaments, and the Koran for better understanding of what the three major faiths of the Middle East believe.

Bibliography

Supplementary to primary resource materials such as interviews and personal correspondence, we consulted a wide range of periodicals and books.

Few of these books are available in general bookstores. Books in print having a Christian orientation may usually be purchased from Christian book dealers; however, works dealing exclusively with a denomination may only be available from the headquarters or missionary department of that denomination.

Some evangelical publishers and religious bookstores may not carry books which deal with theological views and biblical interpretations contrary to their own. Some authors of books on biblical prophecy and interpretation of events in the Middle East may give scant attention to other interpretations. To understand the whole eschatological picture on the Middle East, researchers should examine works by reputable authors on all sides.

Specialized books and recommended reading lists relating to the interest of particular countries may be obtained from the public affairs departments of the embassies of Middle Eastern countries. Again, researchers should recognize that such writings may not give a well-rounded exposition and analysis of controversial events. Embassies represent their particular countries and are concerned with promoting the best image possible to the world. We do not wish to imply that any embassy, Arab or Israeli, promotes deliberate error, but only to observe that interpretations are usually given that support respective national viewpoints, while conflicting and / or differing ideas may be omitted or only briefly mentioned.

We have not attempted to present a chapter-by-chapter bibliography or to include footnotes. Still, readers can be assured that as experienced writers we have been careful to check the validity of source content, whether from printed works, personal interviews, or letters from close-up observers and authorities.

Finally, we have not tried to classify or grade books by our own tastes. Let each researcher decide for himself. We have, though, tried to be helpful by identifying relevant subject matter presented in a particular book. Code letter(s) are given at the end of each entry as follows:

A   Arabs today
Ah Arab history
I   Israel
J   Jewish history
C   Christianity today
Ch Christian history
I   Islam today
Ih Islamic history
B   Biblical interpretation and doctrine
H   History, general
Cu Current events
R   Reference, general

PERIODICALS

Arab Report, Arab Information Report, Washington, D.C., November 1, 1977.

Baptist and Reflector, Tennessee Baptist Convention, Nashville, August 21, 1975, January 19, 1978.

China's Millions, China Inland Mission, London, May 1913.

Christianity Today, Christianity Today Inc., Selected Issues from 1964 through April 1978.

The Commission, The Foreign Mission Board of the Southern Baptist Convention, Richmond, Virginia, Selected Issues from 1972 through April 1978.

Bibliography

Christian Times, Tyndale House Publishers, Wheaton, Illinois, August 20 and September 10, 1967, June 16, 1968.

Christian Living, David C. Cook Publishing Co., Elgin, Illinois, December 5, 1971.

Decision, The Billy Graham Evangelistic Association, Minneapolis, Minnesota, April 1972, March 1977.

Eternity, Evangelical Ministries Inc., Philadelphia, Pennsylvania, Selected Issues from 1972 through April 1978.

Events, Newsmagazine of the Middle East, Beirut and London, December 20, 1977 and January 13, 1978.

Faith at Work, Word Inc., Waco, Texas, December 1972.

His, Intervarsity Christian Fellowship, Downers Grove, Illinois, December 1977.

Home Missions, The Home Mission Board of the Southern Baptist Convention, Atlanta, February 1966, September 1973.

Horizons, The Conservative Baptist Foreign Mission Society, Wheaton, Illinois, January/February 1978.

Interlit, David C. Cook Foundation, Elgin, Illinois, September 1975, December 1977.

Jews for Jesus Newsletter, San Rafael, California, Selected Issues from 1977 through 1978.

Mennonite Central Committee News Service, Akron, Pennsylvania, Releases for 1976, 1977.

Moody Monthly, Moody Bible Institute, Chicago, Illinois, Selected Issues from 1974 through April 1978.

Muslim World Pulse, Evangelical Missions Information Service, Wheaton, Illinois, April 1972, February 1977.

National Geographic, National Geographic Society, Washington, D.C., July 1972.

News Bulletin of Evangelism International, Atlanta, Georgia, Selected Issues 1976 through April 1978.

Newsletter MARC, World Vision International, Pasadena, California, March 1978.

New Wine Magazine, Christian Growth Ministries, Fort Lauderdale, Florida, Special issue on prophecy, January 1977.

Pat Robertson's Perspective, Christian Broadcasting Network, Norfolk, Virginia, December 1977.

The Pentecostal Evangel, The Assemblies of God, Springfield, Missouri, November 27, 1977.

Power, Scripture Press Publications, Inc., Wheaton, Illinois, March 11, 1973, February 16, 1975.

Reader's Digest, The Reader's Digest Association, Pleasantville, New York, Selected Issues, 1970 through April 1978.

Review and Expositor, "The Revival of Apocalyptic," Published by the Faculty of the Southern Baptist Theological Seminary, Louisville, Kentucky, Summer 1975.

Sunday Digest, David C. Cook Publishing Co., Elgin, Illinois, May 5, 1974.

The Alliance Witness, The Christian Missionary Alliance, Nyack, New York, Selected Excerpts and Issues 1943 through 1948 and 1974 through 1977.

The American Jewish Committee Institute of Human Relations' News New York, New York, December 3, 1972.

The Arab League in Today's World, London, December 1976.

The Baptist Standard, Baptist Standard Publishing Co., Dallas, February 8, 1978.

The Chosen People, American Board of Missions to the Jews, Inc., Selected Issues from 1973 through 1975.

The Christian Century, Chicago, Illinois, February 15, 1978.

The Evangelical Beacon, The Evangelical Free Church, Minneapolis, Minnesota, December 16, 1969.

The Everlasting Nation, International Board of Jewish Missions, Inc., Chattanooga, Tennessee, Selected Issues from 1977 through January-February 1978.

The Link, Americans for Middle East Understanding, New York, New York, Selected Issues from 1970 through December 1977.

The Logos Journal, Logos International, Plainfield, New Jersey, Selected Issues from 1977 through January-February 1978.

The Midnight Call, Midnight Call Inc., Hamilton, Ohio, April 1978.

Time, Time Incorporated, New York, New York, Selected Issues from 1947 through April 1978.

U.S. News and World Report, Washington, D.C., Selected Issues from November 1977 through April 1978.

Visions of Apocalypse Rise Again, Russell Chandler and John Dart, reprinted from the *Los Angeles Times,* July 26, 1976.

World Mission Journal, Baptist Brotherhood Commission of the Southern Baptist Convention, Memphis, Tennessee, Selected Issues from 1974 through 1977.

World Vision, World Vision International, Pasadena, California, December 1966, May 1969, June 1969, April 1975, October 1976.

Your Good Neighbor, Radio Bible Hour, Orlando, Florida, September 1976.

BOOKS

Abboushi, W.F., *The Angry Arabs*, The Westminister Press, Philadelphia, 1974. (A, Ah)

Anderson, Per-Olow, *They are Human Too . . . A Photo-Essay on the Palestine Arab Refugees*, Henry Regnery Co., Chicago, 1957. (A)

Antonious, George, *The Arab Awakening*, Capricorn Books, New York, New York n.d. (A, Ah)

Atlas of the Bible Lands, Hammond Inc., Maplewood, New Jersey (B)

Barnhouse, Donald Grey, *Revelation—"God's Last Word,"* Zondervan Publishing House, Grand Rapids, Michigan, 1971. (B)

Barton, James L., *Daybreak in Turkey*, The Pilgrim Press, Boston, 1908. (Ch, Ih)

Ben-Gurion, David, *Israel: Years of Challenge*, Holt Rinehart and Winston, New York, New York, 1963. (I, J)

Bradt, Charles E., King, William R., Rehard, Herbert W., *Around the World: Studies and Stories of Presbyterian Foreign Missions*, The Missionary Press, Wichita, 1912. (Ch)

Brockelmann, Carl, *History of the Islamic Peoples*, Capricorn Books, New York, New York, 1960. (Ih)

Buber, Martin, *Kingship of God*, Translated by Richard Scheimann, 1st American Edition, Harper & Row, New York, New York, 1967. (B)

Byng, Edward, *The World of the Arabs*, Little, Brown & Company, Boston, 1944. (A, Ah, I, Ih)

Cheney, Michael, *Big Oil Man*, Ballantine Books, New York, New York, 1958. (A, Ah)

Childers, Erskine B., *Common Sense about the Arab World*, The Macmillan Co., New York, 1960. (A, Ah, I, Ih)

Cragg, Kenneth, *The Call of the Minaret*, Oxford University Press, New York, New York, 1964. (Ch, I, Ih)

Cragg, Kenneth, *The Dome and the Rock*, Jerusalem Studies in Islam, SPCK, London, 1964. (Ah, I, Ih)

DeLoach, Charles, *Seeds of Conflict*, Logos International, Plainfield, New Jersey, 1974. (A, Ah, I, J, B)

Elliot, Elisabeth, *Furnace of the Lord*, Doubleday and Company, New York, 1969. (A, Ah, I, J, C, Ch, Cu)

Flowers From the Valley of Terror, Translated and Edited by Frances Fuller, Baptist Publications, Beirut, Lebanon, 1977. (A, C, Cu)

Fried, Ralph, *Reaching Arabs for Christ*, Zondervan Publishing House, Grand Rapids, Michigan, 1947. (Ch)

Friedlander, Saul and Hussein, Mahamoud, *Arabs and Israelis: A Dialogue*, Holmes & Meier Publishers, Inc., New York, New York, London, 1975. (A, Ah, I, J, H, Cu)

Glover, Robert Hall, *The Progress of World-Wide Missions*, Revised and Enlarged by J. Herbert Kane, Harper & Row, New York, 1960. (Ch)

Halley, Henry H., *Halley's Bible Handbook*, 23rd Edition, Zondervan Publishing House, Grand Rapids, Michigan, 1962. (R)

Hefley, James and Marti, *Where in the World Are the Jews Today?* Victor Books, Wheaton, Illinois, 1974. (I, J, B)

Hefley, James and Marti, *The Liberated Palestinian*, Victor Books, Wheaton, Illinois, 1975. (A, I, C)

Hirschman, Ira, *Questions and Answers about Arabs and Jews*, Bantam Books, New York, 1977. (I, J, Cu)

Hitti, Philip K., *History of the Arabs*, 9th Edition, St. Martin's Press, New York, New York, 1967. (Ah)

Hitti, Philip K., *History of Syria*, The Macmillan Co., New York, 1959. (Ah)

Hunting, Joseph, *Israel—A Modern Miracle*, Vol. 1, "Prophecies Fulfilled in the Land," The David Press, Murrumbeena, Australia, 1969. (I, J, B, Cu)

Hussein, King of Jordan, *Uneasy Lies the Head*, Bernard Geis Associates, New York, 1962. (A, Ah)

Israel, Time Inc., New York, 1962. (I, J, Cu)

Israel and the Palestinians: A Different Israeli View, A Symposium, Breira Inc., New York, New York. (A, Ah, I, J, Cu)

Jacobsen, Henry, *Bible Knowledge: A Commentary on Romans*, Scripture Press Inc., Wheaton, Illinois. (B)

Kligerman, Aaron J., *The Gospel and the Jew*, Some Collected Writings, Edited by Bernard B. Gair, 1969, privately published. (I, J, Ch, B)

Jordan, Jordan Information Bureau, Amman, Jordan, Summer 1976, Fall 1977. (Ac, Ah)

Kiernan, Thomas, *Arafat: The Man and the Myth*, W.W. Norton & Co., Inc., New York, 1976. (A, Ah, Cu)

Ladd, George E., *A Commentary on the Revelation of John*, Wm. B. Eerdmans, Grand Rapids, Michigan, 1972. (B)

Ladd, George E., *Jesus and the Kingdom*, 1st Edition, Harper & Row, New York, 1964. (B)

LaHaye, Tim, *Revelation Illustrated and Made Plain*, Revised

Edition, Zondervan Publishing House, Grand Rapids, Michigan 1975. (B)

Landau, Rom, *The Arab Heritage of Western Civilization*, Arab Information Center, New York, New York, 1962. (Ah, H)

Lilienthal, Alfred M., *The Other Side of the Coin*, The Devin-Adair Co., New York, 1965. (A, Ah, I, J)

Lindsey, Hal with C.C. Carlson, *The Late Great Planet Earth*, Zondervan Publishing House, Grand Rapids, Michigan, 1970. (I, J, Ch, B, Cu)

Menhun, Moshe, *The Decadence of Judaism in Our Time*, Exposition Press, New York, New York, 1965. (I, J)

Miladin, George, C., *Is This Really the End? (A Reformed Analysis of "The Late Great Planet Earth")*, Mack Publishing Co., Cherry Hill, New Jersey, 1972. (I, J, B, Cu)

Miller, William, *Ten Muslims Meet Christ*, William B. Eerdmans Publishing Co., Grand Rapids, Michigan, 1969. (C, I)

Mission Handbook: North American Protestant Ministries Overseas, Edited by Edward R. Dayton, Missions Advanced Research and Communication Center, A Division of World Vision International, Monrovia, California, 10th Edition, 1973. (C, Ch)

Mundus Artium, A Journal of International Literature and the Arts, Vol. X, Special Arabic Issue, University of Texas Press, Dallas, (A, Ah)

Neve, J.L., *A History of Christian Thought*, The Muhlenberg Press, Philadelphia, 1946. (Ch)

Newell, William R., *Romans Verse by Verse*, Moody Press, Chicago, 1938.

Palestine and the Bible, Mehdi, M.T., Editor, New World Press, New York, 1970. (I, J, B)

Patai, Raphael and Wing, Jennifer P., *The Myth of the Jewish Race*, Charles Scribner's Sons, New York, 1975. (I, J)

Perspective on Palestinian Arabs and Israeli Jews, Edited by James J. Zogby, Medina Press, Wilmette, Illinois, 1977. (A, Ah, I, J, Cu)

Questing in Galilee, The Foreign Mission Board of the Southern Baptist Convention, Richmond, Virginia, 1937.

Richter, Julius, *A History of Protestant Missions in the Near East*, Fleming H. Revell Co., 1910. (Ch)

Rosen, Moishe with William Proctor, *Jews for Jesus*, Fleming H. Revell Co., Inc., 1974. (J, C, B)

Ryrie, Charles C., *The Bible and Tomorrow's News*, Scripture Press

Publications, Inc., Wheaton, Illinois, 1971. (I, J, B, Cu)

Sadat, Anwar, *A Search for Identity*, Harper & Row, New York, New York, 1978.

Signs and Wonders in Rabbath-Ammon, Privately published by S.B. Kawar, Amman, Jordan. n.d. (Ac, Ch)

Smith, Wilbur M., *You Can Know the Future*, Gospel Light Publications, Glendale, California, 1971. (A, Ah, I, J, B)

Snow, Peter, *Hussein*, Robert B. Luce, Inc., Washington, New York, 1972. (A, Ah)

Stagg, Frank, *The Book of Acts*, Broadman Press, Nashville, 1955. (J, B)

Strauss, Lehman, *The Book of the Revelation*, Loizeaux Brothers, Neptune, New Jersey, 1964. (B)

Summers, Ray, *Worthy Is the Lamb*, Broadman Press, Nashville, 1951. (B)

Tatford, Frederick, *The Climax of the Ages: Studies in the Prophecy of Daniel*, Zondervan Publishing House, Grand Rapids, Michigan, 1953. (B)

The Arab World, Time Inc., New York, 1962. (A, Ah, Cu)

The Columbia Encyclopedia, Columbia University Press, New York and London, 1963. (R)

The International Standard Bible Encyclopedia, Wm. B. Eerdmans Publishing Co., Grand Rapids, Michigan, 1949. (R)

The Koran, Translated by J.M. Rodwell, Everyman's Library, Dutton, New York, New York, 1909. (Ih)

The Palestinians, Selected Essays, Edited by Hatem I. Hussaini and Fathalla El-Boghdady, Arab Information Center, Washington, D.C., 1976. (A, Ah, Cu)

The Scofield Reference Bible, edited by C.I. Scofield, Oxford University Press, New York, 1909. (I, J, Ch, H, B)

The Universal Jewish Encyclopedia, Vl. 6, Universal Jewish Encyclopedia Co., 1942. (J)

The World Book Encyclopedia, Field Enterprises Educational Corporation, Chicago, 1976. (R)

Toward Peace in Palestine, Edited by Hatem I. Hussainni, Arab Information Center, Washington, D.C., 1975. (A, Ah, I, Cu)

Turki, Fawaz, *The Disinherited, Journal of a Palestinian Exile*, Monthly Review Press, New York, London, 1972. (A, Cu)

Twentieth Century Encyclopedia of Religious Knowledge (An Extension of the New Schaff-Herzog Encyclopedia of Religious

Bibliography

Knowledge), Lefferts A. Loetscher, Editor-in-Chief, two volumes, Baker Book House, Grand Rapids, Michigan, 1955. (R)

Waterfield, Robin E., *Christians In Persia*, Harper & Row, New York, New York, 1973. (Ch)

Watkins, Bradley, *Is the Modern State, Israel, a Fulfillment of Prophecy?*, privately published. (B)

Who is Menachem Begin? The Institute for Palestine Studies, Beirut, 1977. (I, J)

Your Muslim Guest, Fellowship of Faith for Muslims, Toronto. (C, I)

Zondervan Pictorial Bible Dictionary, Zondervan Publishing House, 1963.

For free information on how to receive
the international magazine

LOGOS JOURNAL

also Book Catalog

Write: Information - LOGOS JOURNAL CATALOG
Box 191
Plainfield, NJ 07061